MAKING
YOUR MONEY
WORK FOR
YOUR FUTURE

2

MAKING YOUR MONEY WORK FOR YOUR FUTURE

PAUL LEWIS

LIFEGUIDES

AUTHOR

Paul Lewis is the presenter of BBC Radio 4's *Money Box* and many of the *Money Box Live* phone-ins, as well as other programmes covering personal finance issues. He also appears regularly on BBC1's *Breakfast*. He contributes a column to *Saga Magazine*, is the author of various personal finance leaflets and has written several books. His website is www.paullewis.co.uk.

This guide contains a great deal of financial information which, like all such information, may go out of date. Before making money-related decisions, it may be wise to check the latest information at source (contact details are given throughout the text and in chapter 14).

LifeGuides are commissioned and published by Help the Aged, 207–221 Pentonville Road, London N1 9UZ and can be purchased via www.helptheaged.org.uk or from bookshops

For a full list of Help the Aged publications, see the website, telephone 020 7239 1946 or email publications@helptheaged.org.uk

First published 2008

Copyright © 2008 Help the Aged

Trade distribution by Turnaround Publisher Services Ltd

British Library Cataloguing in Publication Data
A catalogue record for this book is available from the British Library

ISBN 978-1-84598-028-3

Designed and typeset by Price Watkins Design
Printed and bound in England by CPI Mackay Ltd

CONTENTS

CONTENTS, continued

1

INTRODUCTION

INTRODUCTION

This book is about the second half of your life, which it counts from the age of 50. Now strictly speaking that isn't the second half of your life. At 50 you have about 30 years left on average – a few months more if you are a man, more than three years if you are a woman. So you have around 40 per cent of your life left rather than 50 per cent. But the way things are going, those figures are very pessimistic (if you believe that longer life is a Good Thing, which most of us do). Every year life expectancy grows by about three months. So by the time you reach 80 you will probably still have a good few years left. There is more later on longevity and how it is becoming more prevalent.

So when this book says 'middle life', it starts at 50.

The years at the start of the second half of your life can be good or bad. They are usually different.

Today's fiftysomethings in the UK face a longer life ahead than they have at any time in history. But as your 50s pass you know with growing certainty that you are *more than halfway*.

Of course, that is only generally true. Jeanne Calment, a Frenchwoman, died at the record age of 122 in 1997. She lived in Arles in south-west France and could remember meeting Van Gogh in her mother-in-law's shop. Her halfway point came after her 50s were but a memory. But she was a record-breaker – and if she had given up smoking before she was 120 she might still be around today.

So, because you are almost certainly beyond halfway, everything you do has to count – and there's not a moment to lose.

THE ROAD AHEAD

We are all different and we all lead different lives, so it is difficult to say what is typical. Some people in their 50s are in the stereotypical family of the adverts and sit-coms, where the house is paid for, the kids are becoming independent, money is easier, debts are paid off, holidays beckon and retirement is looked forward to. Others lose their job, have to look after ailing relatives, find their arthritis is getting worse, have growing debts and know that their pension will barely be enough to live on.

This book will show what choices you have and what dangers there are ahead. If you read it and follow at least some of the advice in it you will be better off for the rest of your life – guaranteed. It is not too late to take steps to have more money in retirement.

People (usually rich ones) say that money is not the key to happiness. But not having enough can take you a long way down the road to misery. So this book is about money: money in your 50s and beyond – not as a route to happiness, but at least as the solution to one of the potential problems of later life.

Money and how much you have depends on all sorts of other things – work, luck, relationships, death and taxes. So it will touch on these non-financial topics too as we pass by.

There will inevitably be some arithmetic in it.

Some people like arithmetic. Most people do not. So there is a minimum of arithmetic in this book. Fortunately the arithmetic of personal finance does not need to deal with much more than having a fiver in your pocket and spending various amounts from 10p to £20 (leaving you with either £4.90 or a £15 debt).

FIRST PRINCIPLES FOR MAXIMISING INCOME

Let us start with the blindingly obvious. To end up with more money you have two choices: get more or spend less. This book is divided into those two parts, each dealing with one of those choices. However, some things fall into both parts – borrowing and tax, for example – and just a few, such as divorce, are in a third section. That is the trouble with the human desire to classify things. It brings great rewards but there are always those odd items that you stuff into any old drawer to get them out of the way.

Now, as Mao said, the longest journey starts with a single step –

and the most important thing before you embark on any journey is to know where you are now. It is no use setting off for the hills of wealth if you do not realise you have to climb out of the caves of debt first. (There will be a bit of flowery language from time to time, just to bring a smile to your lips and offset all the numbers.) As there is no GPS (global positioning system) for personal finance you have to sit down and look at money in and money out and see how that might change when at some point in the foreseeable future you might just want to ease off a bit and earn less.

So financial planning begins with you writing down your income, what you spend your money on, what debts you have (yes, do include the mortgage), what pension you pay into, any investments you have, any savings . . . and so on. And if you have a partner and share your finances, you both need to do it – and be honest with each other.

Stuff happens, all your life. But in the second half big changes loom that can affect your money – and every other area of your life.

Normally income goes down, although for some there is a golden period when pay goes up as retirement approaches.

Debts may reduce. But if income does fall, the temptation to spend a bit more than you earn can be overwhelming.

If you have children, they tend to become financially independent. But there is always that bill for the wedding and the plea for help to buy that first home.

Redundancy affects many people in their 50s. Although it is now unlawful to discriminate on the grounds of age, employers still find it an attractive option.

Separation and divorce continue to grow among the over-50s. Ending a relationship is always traumatic. When this happens in later life it can be devastating.

Caring for older relatives can creep up on you in this half of your life. Often it is not the person you expect who ends up dependent.

All these things will be looked at in more detail in the book. But as the business gurus often tell us, every threat can be turned into an opportunity.

And the key message of this guide is that it's *not* too late:

- **not too late** to plan for a better pension
- **not too late** to sort out your debts
- **not too late** to change your job or start a new one
- **not too late** to save some money.

And above all it is not **too late** to change those bad money habits. So welcome to making your money work for your future. ■

PART I

BOOSTING INCOME

It may seem obvious but the best way to have more money is to increase your income. This part looks at how to do just that. Some of the ideas are straightforward – work more and earn more. Others are about making sure that the money you have paid in taxes all your life now comes back in benefits to you. And a big chunk is about making your money work hard – as hard as you worked for it in the first place. Making your money work by sensible saving and cautious investing is an important element in having a higher income. If all else fails, look around you: the bricks and mortar that you live in can be used to raise money either directly or indirectly. After all, you bought it in the first place: why shouldn't that wealth keep you now?

2
WORK

WORK

Many people believe that working more, harder or better is the best way to increase income. OK. They are puritans. And of course, where work is concerned it is not always that simple. As the years advance it can become more difficult to change jobs, get promotion or boost your pay. So this section looks at your rights at work and how self-employment can mean self-empowerment.

EMPLOYMENT

At your age you have probably gone through the process of getting a job several times. But last time was probably some time ago and lots of things have changed. So let us pretend you have never done it before and see what happens.

Sit yourself at your computer. Start a document headed 'My skills' and make a list of what you have done and what you can do. Don't be shy. Don't start with the exams you passed at school. No one cares about those, not least because any talk of O-levels or CSEs just makes you seem old. So always start with the most recent things you have done and work backwards. Don't just include things you have done at work. Bringing up three children? Acting as chair of the local allotment society? Running a charity collection at the kids' last sports day? Organising the pub quizzes? And of course, using a computer to write what is conventionally called your CV, or *curriculum vitae* – a list of the things you have done in your life.

These are all skills – useful skills for an employee.

Then put down the things you did at work – responsibilities you had, special posts you held, particular achievements, and yes, you should include that first aid qualification.

Finally, list those dull old exams you took and did well at before anyone could cheat with a calculator or a mobile phone.

Then talk to your partner, colleagues and friends about it. They will probably all have something to contribute: 'Didn't you spend some time in the parent teacher association when your Mel was at school?' 'Wasn't it you who was the fire warden for five years before, you know, that weird bloke with the centre parting took over?' 'You must mention that idea you had which saved them thousands and they never gave you any credit.'

Add these things in the appropriate place. That's why a computer is so much better than a piece of paper.

Read it. That's you. Good, isn't it? That's step one. Selling your life to yourself. When you need to send off your CV for a real job add things relevant to that particular task, a job which, of course, you have always wanted to do, matching the skills the employer is looking for to what you have done in your life.

But the purpose of this book isn't to tell you how to apply for a job. It's to tell you about the money.

Let's start at the bottom.

MINIMUM WAGE

From 1 October 2007 everyone working in the UK had to be paid at least £5.52 an hour, which means, for a 40-hour week, £220.80 or £11,481 a year. Not a lot, is it? But it has been a useful yardstick for wages since it was introduced in April 1999. If you are paid less than that it is unlawful (although there are lower rates for people under 22) and HM Revenue & Customs would like to know about it.

Although the National Minimum Wage sounds simple, it can get complicated. The official guidance runs to 132 pages.

If you are in a job where tips are given, the tips can be counted as part of your pay only if they are paid as part of the bill and included in your pay. Tips given to you directly – even if they are collected and divided up – do not count towards the minimum wage. (That is why it is always better for staff if you leave a tip in cash rather than accept the invitation on the credit card machine to add one there.)

You are entitled to 24 days' paid leave during the year, so your hourly pay at work has to reflect that. Note that the 24 days includes bank holidays. Until October 2007 it was 20 days and it will rise to 28 days – including bank holidays – in April 2009. What this means is that if you work in a temporary job the hourly pay has to reflect the time off. You should be paid £6.08 an hour to do that.

If you are not paid per hour but per item there are complex rules about how you fairly work out your average pay over a 40-hour week which must be at least the minimum wage.

If your job requires you to travel, the time it takes is part of your working week, with the exception of the time it takes you to get from your home to your work.

If you work in agriculture your pay is controlled, according to a rather more complicated system, by the Agricultural Wages Board. But it will be at least as much as the minimum wage.

To find out more, go to: www.direct.gov.uk/en/Employment/Employees/Pay/DG_10027201
National Minimum Wage helpline: 08456 000 678
www.hmrc.gov.uk/nmw

If you have a very low income, you need to be aware of tax credits (see page 48) and the other benefits available, which are covered in chapter 3.

NATIONAL INSURANCE

If you are working part-time there is crucial pay level, £90 a week (in 2008/9), that represents a fraction over 16 hours' work at the minimum wage. Once you earn £90 a week you start getting credits for National Insurance contributions. However, you do not have to pay them until your pay rises to £105 a week. The contributions are 11 per cent of your pay above £105 a week. So on £125 a week you will pay £2.20 in National Insurance. On £250 a week you will pay £15.95. The best deal, of course, is to earn between £90 and £105 so that you get the contributions credited but do not have to pay anything.

National Insurance contributions give you several important rights.

1 If you lose your job and are actively looking for work you may get Jobseeker's Allowance. That is £60.50 a week and lasts for 26 weeks. After that it becomes means-tested – and if you have a partner you live with that test is applied to your joint income, which scuppers the claims made by many people who live with someone else. To qualify at all you have to have paid full National Insurance contributions for two tax years before – roughly – the calendar year in which you claim.

2 You will normally qualify for statutory sick pay from your employer if you are off work due to illness. Statutory Sick Pay is £75.40 a week and lasts 28 weeks. Your employer pays it (after you have had three days off sick) and you get it only if you are earning more than £90 a week. Statutory Sick Pay does not depend on your National Insurance record, just on your pay. But if you have paid the contributions (or had them credited) and you do not qualify for Statutory Sick Pay – or after it runs out – you can claim Incapacity Benefit, which can last until pension age. Incapacity Benefit has the same contribution conditions as Jobseeker's Allowance.

The rules on getting all these benefits include many complex conditions which there is no space to cover here. But the point is that if you do not earn more than £90 a week you will not be credited with or pay National Insurance contributions, and that will stop you getting some of them at all even if you have been working for a long time.

3 National Insurance contributions count towards your state retirement pension. Some people of course already have a full state pension. If you reach pension age on or after 6 April 2010 you will need only 30 years' contributions to get a full state pension. Many people will not have paid enough contributions by the time they are 50 to get a full pension, so every year of contributions they add on will mean more money after pension age. One small point that annoys people now and will annoy them even more after 2010 is that National Insurance contributions still have to be paid even if you have paid enough to get a full retirement pension. They do not stop once you have reached that magic 30 (it is more now: 39 for women and 44 for men, so it is not so much of an issue). In that sense those extra contributions are wasted.

TWO OR MORE JOBS?
If you have more than one job then you must make sure that the
National Insurance contributions you pay are correct. Here is the
problem. You pay the full rate on earnings between £90 and £770 a
week (£4,680 and £40,040 a year) and 1 per cent on earnings above
that. If you just have one job that is easy to work out. Those rates
apply on your total earnings from all jobs you may have. If you have
two or more jobs each employer has to know about the other jobs
otherwise you could end up paying too little or too much. So make
sure all your employers know about the other employers.

MARRIED WOMEN
This book is about earning more and spending less. But it is time for
a little diversion to talk directly to a small and shrinking group, the
32,000 married women who still pay the so-called reduced Married Woman's National Insurance contributions. **Those contributions
are a waste of money**. They are 4.85 per cent of your earnings
between £105 a week and £770 a week and 1 per cent above that.
So some women are paying £32.25 a week or more in **useless contributions**.

To make it absolutely clear: **these contributions get you no
benefits.** So why do some women pay them? A bit of history will
explain (see box overleaf).

Slowly the numbers of women paying the Married Woman's
Stamp have diminished. Some have reached pension age and stopped
paying contributions. Others have had two whole tax years out of the
labour market, at which time the right to pay reduced-rate contributions disappears. More still have switched to full contributions – some
after they have read advice given in the media advising them to **pay
full contributions.**

Fortunately, there are now, reportedly, only about 32,000 of them
left. Among them are a very few people for whom switching to full
contributions is bad advice. But for almost everyone else it is really
good advice:

MARRIED WOMAN'S STAMP

When the National Insurance system began in 1948 most adults lived in couples and married women tended to be financially dependent on their husband. His pension contributions paid for a pension for her too – at 60 per cent of the full rate – and so if she did work there was no point in her paying for a pension as well. So the Married Woman's Stamp was born. From May 1977 it was sort of stopped. Any woman who started work after that had to pay the full National Insurance contributions. But anyone working at the time could carry on paying these worthless contributions – and millions did.

1 For every year you pay full contributions you are earning some State Second Pension (find out more about that on page 46). That is enough in itself to make paying them worthwhile. The only exceptions are married women who are members of a good pension scheme at work which links their pension to their pay. They will not earn State Second Pension.

2 For every year you pay you are building up a bigger entitlement to a basic state pension. Some people will find that does not benefit them. They are (a) women who are younger than their husbands by five years or more and whose pension entitlement could never be more than the pension they could get as a married woman on his contributions; and (b) women born before 6 April 1952 who cannot build up at least ten years' contributions.

3 After a couple of years you will be able to claim Jobseeker's Allowance or Incapacity Benefit if you lose your job or become too ill or disabled to work.

4 If you subsequently take time off to care for a child of yours or for a relative you may be able to get those years counted towards your state pension. After two years of caring or looking after a child the years should count anyway (but see page 43 on state pension).

So it's win-win-win-win in almost every case. You change from reduced-rate to full-rate contributions by using a form called CF9, which you can download from the HM Revenue & Customs website at www.hmrc.gov.uk/forms/cf9.pdf. The change takes effect immediately, so you will start paying full National Insurance contributions at once. Whether you will pay enough to count in the current year depends on what you earn and how much of the tax year is left. But if it does not count you will be able to make it count by paying voluntary contributions. You can do that up to six years later. Also, in case you were wondering – no, you cannot pay voluntary contributions while you are still entitled to pay the reduced Married Woman's Contribution.

PENSION AGE

After all that complexity here is something nice and simple. Once you reach pension age you do not have to pay National Insurance contributions at all. At the moment pension age for men is 65 while for women it is 60. So in the week of your 60th birthday if you are a woman, or your 65th birthday if you are a man, you should not pay contributions and you will never have to pay them again. And considering they are 11 per cent of a big chunk of your pay, that is a big saving. Things are slightly more complicated for self-employed people (see below).

Women born after 5 April 1952 will reach pension age after they reach 60 so will have to carry on paying National Insurance contributions for a bit longer until they reach the age when they can draw their pension. There is more about the changing pension age for women on page 45. Pension age will change for men too, eventually, so men who are well under 50 should also turn to that page.

AGE DISCRIMINATION

Since 1 October 2006 discriminating against people on grounds of age in employment and training has been unlawful. But then, so is using a mobile phone while driving – and one in three drivers admits to doing that.

Although the law exists it is up to society, not the police, to enforce it. Like all discrimination laws, this one is developing as people go to court to test out exactly what it means. So if you feel you have been discriminated against in the field of employment on grounds of age it is always worth complaining, and pursuing it further if you are not happy with the answer.

The law is supposed to protect you from discrimination all through employment starting with recruitment. However, there are three areas where the government will allow discrimination on grounds of age. It says these exceptions are allowed under the European law which the age discrimination rules implement.

Minimum wage There are three rates of the minimum wage depending on the employee's age – under 18, 18–21 and 22 and over. A challenge to the legality of this age scale is currently going through the courts.

Redundancy pay There are also three age-related rates of redundancy pay. For those under the age of 22 each year spent working for an employer who makes you redundant entitles you to half a week's pay. Those aged 22 to 40 are entitled to one week's pay per year worked, and those aged 41 or more are entitled to one and a half week's pay per year worked. The government has decided those age bands are lawful under the age discrimination rules. Your employer may pay more than these amounts and discriminate on grounds of age as long as it adheres to these bands. For example, it may give twice these amounts or substitute a month's pay for a week's (for more on redundancy see pages 195–9).

Retirement age An employer can specify that all its employees retire at a certain age provided that that age is at least 65 and the policy applies to every employee. However, there are strict rules about how this rule is implemented. Your employer cannot just tuck your P45 inside your 65th birthday card. First, you must be given at least six months' notice before you reach 65 that you will be expected to retire then. Second, you have the right to ask to work longer. The employer must consider that request and give you a response within a reasonable time period. You can then ask for that decision to be reviewed. Only when all that has been done can your boss make you go. But at each stage all he or she has to do to comply with the law is to say 'that is our policy'.

These rules are currently the subject of a legal challenge to the European Court of Justice, with a decision expected by 2009, and the government has promised to review the rules in 2011. With state pension age rising to 66 in 2024 and to 68 by 2044 it seems unlikely that this discrimination will survive forever.

COMPANY PENSION
Company pension schemes are largely exempt from the age discrimination rules. Schemes can set age limits for joining a scheme, and can have different pensions for existing staff and new staff, vary contributions by age, and set an age at which contributions to the scheme must stop and at which the pension may be drawn. So although an individual might work until, say, the age of 75, the last ten years may not count towards their pension. The law now allows you to draw your company pension and carry on working full-time for the same company. But your scheme may not allow that.

APPLYING FOR JOBS
It is now generally unlawful to choose or reject a person for a job on grounds of their age. Although you may see job adverts that specify 'young person', 'mature person' or even 'eager to learn' all those words can be interpreted as an intention to discriminate against older or younger people. And anyone rejected for such a job could go to a tribunal and claim discrimination on grounds of age.

A job application form should not normally ask for your age – though an employer can ask for your age or date of birth on a separate form to 'monitor diversity'. But if the employer does that it cannot be used as part of the selection process. One recent case in Ireland – which like the UK introduced age discrimination laws to comply with a European Directive – held that someone who was asked their age on a form was entitled to lie about it and could not be refused the job on the grounds that he had lied.

AT WORK

Once you are in a job, any decisions on your future should not be made on grounds of age. Promotion or other advances in your career should not be related to your age. And nor should decisions to hold you back. You should be given equal access to training or career development regardless of your age. The only exception might be if you are approaching the company's fixed retirement age and the benefit the employer would get from training you would be insufficient to justify it.

Pay should generally not be related to age. And because length of service is indirectly related to age – the longer you have been in a job, the older you will be – pay cannot normally be related to length of service either. However, there are two exceptions:

1 employers can give you a pay rise for being in the job as long as that happens within five years of your starting it

2 employers will be able to pay more to long-serving staff who have been with the company for more than five years if they can show there are good reasons for doing so: for example, if experience makes staff work more quickly and efficiently or if it helps retain staff who might otherwise look for another job.

Full employment rights now extend to anyone of any age. So if your employer lets you work beyond the age of 65 you cannot be dismissed without good reason. In the past you could be dismissed without a reason once you were 65. Now, employers who want to dismiss someone over 65 will have to take care to do it fairly. Older people can of course be dismissed for the normal reasons, such as incompetence or dishonesty; they can also be made redundant; but no one can be picked for redundancy on grounds of age.

If someone over 65 is made redundant they are entitled to a redundancy payment. Before the law changed in 2006 they got nothing. If you suspect you have been selected for redundancy on grounds of age you may have a clear case of discrimination and could seek compensation.

OBJECTIVE JUSTIFICATION

There is one big loophole in the new law. An employer may discriminate on grounds of age if such discrimination can be 'objectively justified'. For example, a company that wanted to fix a retirement age of 55 for a particular job would have to show that to do the task required certain physical or mental abilities which people over that age do not have. Because people age at different rates it will be hard to prove that such justification exists. But 'objective justification' is likely to be the big battleground between employers who want to discriminate on grounds of age and their staff who object.

OUTSIDE WORK

The new laws apply to paid employees but do not cover volunteers. However, they do extend a little way beyond the workplace. All colleges and universities have to admit people regardless of their age. However, if you do a degree course you will not get a student loan for your living costs unless you are under 60. The government insists that this age bar is also fully in accordance with the new law. Strangely, though, you can get a loan to pay your tuition fees (up to £3,000 a year) at any age and there is no bar to older people benefiting from the various grants now available.

At the moment age discrimination regulations do not extend beyond work and training. So if you are not allowed in a club or you are refused insurance or a credit card because you are too old that is not unlawful. However, the government is consulting on whether it should be and eventually it is inevitable that it will become unlawful to discriminate on grounds of age when providing goods or services. Again, however, 'objective justification' is likely to be an area of dispute.

Useful guidance on identifying age stereotyping or discrimination, whether in the workplace where you are employed or during the recruitment process, is in *How to Recognise Cases of Age Discrimination*, available at: www.taen.org.uk/publications/ad_guide_for_workers.pdf (see especially page 44).

WHAT TO DO ABOUT AGE DISCRIMINATION

Anyone who thinks they have been discriminated against on grounds of age should first complain to their employer. Talk to your immediate boss or to the personnel or human resources department, if there is one. Explain why you think you have been discriminated against and what you would like to happen. If that does not work you could consult Citizens Advice or an employment lawyer about the possibility of going to an employment tribunal. The tribunal can order the employer to pay compensation and to reinstate someone who has been unlawfully dismissed.

Always get advice before complaining to an employment tribunal. Find out more from www.employmenttribunals.gov.uk.

You can also complain to the Equality and Human Rights Commission, which brings together the previous commissions for sex, race and disability discrimination and adds to it the three further discriminations on grounds of sexual orientation, religious belief and age. Find out more at www.equalityhumanrights.com. The Commission does not extend to Northern Ireland.

GOING IT ALONE

Here is an interesting fact. As you get older you become less attractive as an employee – but more attractive as a consultant. In other words, if – despite the discrimination laws – you find it too difficult to get a job or promotion or to make a new start, one possibility is self-employment.

Twenty years ago there was no formality about it at all. One day you were an employee working for your employer. The next you were sitting at home thinking 'What have I done?' and ringing round begging for work. But soon there would be half a dozen people willing to pay you money for whatever it was you did and you will never have looked back.

Today you have to register as self-employed or risk being fined £100. You have three months to register from the end of the month in which you started to be self-employed. And if you do not do it by October in the tax year after you start to be self-employed further penalties could be due. Registering is simple. You can do it over the phone (0845 9154 515) or through the Revenue's website at: www.hmrc.gov.uk/findout/index.htm, which has lots of information about self-employment.

But are you *really* self-employed? The problem with self-employment is that it can creep up on you. One day you are selling your unwanted Christmas presents on eBay or doing the annual accounts free for the local canal enthusiasts' society. The next you are buying Bunnykins figures to resell them or the local hairdresser is paying you to do her bookkeeping. It would be easier if the Revenue allowed you to earn, say, £5,000 a year before you became self-employed. But it does not. If you are selling your services or buying things to resell them you are self-employed and you have to register or face the penalty – even if you only earn £100 during the year – or make a loss.

So register. Once you have done that the next thing to think about is National Insurance. Strictly speaking, you have to pay what are called Class 2 National Insurance contributions, currently £2.30 a week. Of course, once you reach pension age you need not worry about them. Normally, the last payment is for the week before your birthday. Remember, if you are a woman born on 6 April 1952 or later you reach pension age on a particular date after your birthday (explained later in all its glorious complexity on pages 43– 5). Now if you earn less than £4,825 a year (£92.79 a week) you do not have to pay Class 2. But to avoid them you have to apply for what is called Small Earnings Exception. The form and an explanation in a language similar to English called 'Revenue-ese' is at www.hmrc.gov.uk/forms/cf10.pdf. Class 2 contributions give you entitlement to basic state pension, incapacity benefits, bereavement benefits (for your spouse or civil partner) and maternity benefits. At £2.30 a week that is quite a bargain.

If you earn more than £5,435 a year from self-employment you will have to pay another sort of National Insurance, called Class 4. You pay this with your income tax through the self-assessment form. It is 8 per cent of your profits between £5,435 and £40,040 and 1 per cent of profits above £40,040. (These figures apply in 2008/9 and will change after that.) So it can be quite a lot of money. You get nothing from it. Absolutely nothing. Zilch. Zero. It does not help you qualify for any benefits, nor does it count towards the state pension. Unlike the contributions paid by employees it does not count towards the State Second Pension. It is a tax, and that's it. It also stops at pension age. But in the case of Class 4 it does not stop in the week you reach pension age but at the end of the tax year in which you reach pension age. So if you are a man and reach 65 in 2008/9 your Class 2 contributions will stop on your birthday. But Class 4 will be charged on your profits for the whole year 2008/9.

No, it is neither fair nor logical – but this is tax.

Talking of tax brings us to another point about self-employment. You may have noticed the dreaded words 'self-assessment form' at the top of the page, and yes, once you are self-employed you are not only responsible for finding work, doing it, sending in an invoice, and paying National Insurance contributions, you also have to work out your own income tax and pay it.

SELF-ASSESSMENT AND TAX ALLOWANCES

If your turnover is less than £15,000 you just have to enter your turnover, your expenses and your net profit on the self-assessment form. If your turnover is more than that you have to fill in the full self-assessment form together with the pages for self-employment – they have a pink flash on them. It can seem a bit daunting. There is more about self-assessment later.

If you are self-employed you must keep accurate records. You are taxed on your profit. That is the difference between the money you are paid for the things or services you sell and the money you pay out on your business expenses. Write down everything you spend – even a newspaper or a bus ticket. As long as it is a business expense get a receipt and keep it. And if you buy things to sell, of course the price you pay for them is a business expense.

So far so simple. But of course if your office is in your home and your car is partly for business use and partly for personal use it can get more difficult. For example, if you have a telephone that is not exclusively used for business the business calls – and part of the rental – can be counted as a business expense. You can work out how much by going through your calls at the end of the quarter and seeing how much you spend on business calls and how much on personal calls. Claim the calls and work out the proportion of your calls that relate to business and claim that share of the rental. Do it once and then use the same proportion of your total bill each month. Keep a note of how you worked it out in case the Revenue should ask. If your business grows – or shrinks – you should do the check again.

Use the same technique for the running expenses of your car. Check the mileage for business trips and personal use and then claim the proportion of the petrol, tax, servicing, insurance and breakdown service. And make sure that your insurer knows you are using the car for business on your own account. It probably will not affect your premiums. But if you do not tell the company and you have an accident and make a claim saying 'I was on my way to see a client' the insurer may not pay up.

If you use a room in your home as your office you can charge to the business a share of some of the expenses of running your home. Unfortunately the Revenue has no official list of the expenses you can charge, nor is there any guidance on working out the proportion you can allocate to the business. However, it seems to be accepted that a share of the heating, electricity, Council Tax and the part of the mortgage repayments that represents interest can be charged as can a share of any contents insurance relevant to your business. You can charge part of the water costs only if you have a water meter.

The traditional way of working out the share is to count the number of rooms in your home excluding a bathroom or toilet. Count the rooms used as your office, normally one, and claim that fraction of the costs. See box overleaf.

One danger of using the proportion method is that if you use one room exclusively as an office that room may be subject to Capital Gains Tax when you sell the property. So it is best if it has an additional use – say as a guest room or study.

Until recently the costs of office equipment or a vehicle were dealt with differently. You did not just take them off your profits before working out your tax. Instead, you had to claim what are called 'capital allowances'. They spread the cost of the equipment over a number of years. So if you bought a computer for your business in 2007/8 you could charge 50 per cent of the cost as an expense in the first year and the 25 per cent of the balance every year after that. But that has all been simplified for 2008/9. Each year you get an Annual Investment Allowance of £50,000. If you spend less than that on capital items you can charge the full amount in the year you buy them.

The exception is a vehicle. You can only charge 20 per cent of the cost in the first year and 20 per cent of the balance left in each year after that. There is an upper limit on the value of the car for which you are claiming: £15,000. More generous allowances may be available for energy-efficient vehicles, so do check if you buy one new.

Special rules apply in the first two years of a new business and the year in which it ends. You may need advice about how to work that out.

WORKING OUT WHAT TO CLAIM FOR ON YOUR HOME OFFICE

- If your home has four rooms and your office occupies one, a quarter of the costs can be allocated to the business.
- Alternatively, you can measure the area of your office and of the whole home and use that fraction. But that is likely to give a smaller proportion.

As there are no official rulings, you just need to use a method you think is fair and write down what you have done, so you can justify it if there is an investigation.

You can get more information on business expenses and capital allowances in the Self-assessment Help Sheet IR222 (see chapter 14).

VAT

If the annual turnover of your business is £64,000 or more you will have to register for VAT. This is turnover, remember – the income of your business, not your profit. If you do register, you have to add VAT to all your fees and prices – normally at 17.5 per cent, though some items are charged at 5 per cent and others at 0 per cent – and hand that tax over to HMRC at the end of each quarter. It also means you can deduct from the payment the cost of VAT on anything you have bought for the business. So registering for VAT can save you money as things you buy for the business – from stationery to computers – are effectively free of VAT.

If your turnover excluding VAT is £150,000 or less you can avoid those fiddly sums by registering for the flat-rate VAT scheme. Instead of doing all the calculations each quarter you just hand over a fixed percentage of your turnover including VAT. Those percentages range from 4 per cent to 13.5 per cent depending on your business. The flat-rate scheme saves a lot of time and can save money. Once registered for it you can stick with it until your turnover including VAT exceeds £225,000 – at which point you can probably afford an accountant to sort it all out for you. ■

3
BENEFITS

The best guide to the hugely complex system of benefits for illness, disability, unemployment, bereavement, retirement, maternity, carers, children, tax credits, rent and Council Tax runs to more than 1,500 pages, printed on bible paper and in a type size that would challenge the eyesight of many people, but even that guide does not cover everything. So in just a few short paragraphs this chapter can only give an indication of what you might get.

MEANS-TESTING

Means-testing is one of those bureaucrats' words invented in the 1930s to cover the tests used to see if the 'means' of unemployed people were low enough to entitle them to get help from the state after their initial 'dole' ran out. It was an intrusive and, many felt, an insulting invasion of their privacy. There are still many people today whose folk or family memory of means-testing makes them despise it just as honest working people did in the Depression that preceded World War II. Of course, the government has tried to re-brand means-testing as 'income-related' or even as 'targeting resources'. But the simple fact is that people do not like telling officials about their income, and even less divulging their savings. 'None of their business' is a common cry. That is especially true in small communities where the benefits officer may well be your neighbour's daughter.

It is not just dislike of the means test that puts people off. The whole notion of 'proving your poverty' to get handouts from the state is widely hated. Many people who overcome that are daunted by the complex and unintelligible forms they have to fill in. And others simply do not know that they can get help.

The result is that the government saves many billions of pounds a year which should be helping people with their Council Tax, rent, or living expenses because people who are entitled to extra money in return for filling in a form do not get it. So the mission of this chapter is to get everyone who is entitled to these benefits to claim them.

The phrase 'hideously complex' is barely adequate to describe the rules that govern means-tested – sorry – income-related benefits. The rules change at the age of 60, too, and in some cases again at 65.

First, there is **Council Tax**, recently voted one of the two most hated taxes (the other was inheritance tax – see pages 210–216), which may be reduced using means-testing or without using means-testing. The non-means-tested ways work as follows.

- If you live alone you can get a reduction in your Council Tax of a quarter. So if your tax is £1,000 a year it will be cut to £750. All you have to do is tell the council you live alone. This reduction will be backdated to the time you were first living alone. The council may ask for proof but the electoral register will probably be considered adequate.
- If you have a home which has been adapted for the needs of a disabled resident your Council Tax can be reduced by about 16 per cent. What they actually do is move your home down a band, and if it is already in Band A they cut the tax by a sixth.
- If another adult lives with you who is not your partner or a tenant and their income is less than £220 a week the tax can be cut by between 7.5 per cent and 25 per cent. If the other person is a student it can be cut to zero.

Now comes the difficult bit – **Council Tax Benefit**, which depends on your income and your savings. It also depends on your age and on the amount of your Council Tax. The typical Council Tax for a Band D home in 2008/9 is about £1,400 (that is before any of the deductions mentioned above). If your full tax is £1,400 you can get some reduction if your weekly income is less than £161 a week. Once you reach the magic age of 60 you can get help if your income is up to £224 a week. And once you reach the double magic age of 65 that upper limit rises to £244 a week. The corresponding amounts for a couple are £229 (under 60), £323 (60–64) and £349 for those aged 65 or more). If your income is higher than this do not assume you cannot get anything. Council Tax of more than £1,400 is quite common and if yours is more you can have a higher income and still get help.

Now, just before you rush off to claim there is another problem: savings. If you have money in the bank (or under the mattress) or investments, these can count against you. The way it is done is very odd. The actual income the savings earn is ignored completely. Instead, if your savings exceed £6,000 and you are:

- **aged under 60**, £1 is added to your income and then another £1 is added for every whole £250 savings you have above £6,000. So if you have £10,424 in savings that counts as £18 added to your income.
- **aged 60 or more**, £1 is added to your income and then another £1 for every £500 savings you have above £6,000. So if you have £10,424 in savings that counts as £9 added to your income.

If you have more than £16,000 savings you cannot get Council Tax Benefit at all *except* if you are aged 60 or more *and* get another benefit, called Pension Credit Guarantee Credit, which has no upper limit. Pension Credit and the two parts it comes in – Guarantee Credit and Savings Credit – are explained later on page 42.

Different – and more generous – rules apply in Northern Ireland, where help with the rates (non-Irish readers should note that there is no Council Tax in NI) is available higher up the income scale – over £300 a week in many cases.

If you have followed all this – or even bits of it – why not apply for a cut in your Council Tax? Go to your local council – the one that charges you the tax – and ask about the non-means-tested discounts and about Council Tax Benefit. It could turn out to be (fairly) easy money.

HOUSING BENEFIT

If you pay rent you can get a discount off that too on grounds of low income. The rules for people in council or housing association properties are similar to the ones for Council Tax Benefit. The rules for people with private landlords are, from April 2008, that instead of using the actual rent in the calculation you use a fixed local housing allowance which is the typical rent in the area of the accommodation. The allowance you get may be more or less than the actual rent you pay. Either way you apply to your local council office for the discount in the same way – and usually at the same time – as Council Tax Benefit.

HELP WITH LIVING COSTS

Under 60 If you are under 60 the government will help you with your living costs only if you are either looking for work or you are unable to work because you are a lone parent or have an illness or disability which prevents you from working. If you are in one of those groups your income – including any benefits you may already be getting – will be topped up to £60.50 a week if you are single or £94.95 for a couple. You will also get all your Council Tax paid and most of your rent through Housing Benefit. If you are disabled you may get more. If you live as part of a couple your joint income is counted. Savings are converted to income in the same way as for Council Tax Benefit. If they are more than £16,000 you will not get any help.

Over 60 Once you hit the magic age of 60 you can claim one part of Pension Credit: Guarantee Credit. This will top up your income to £124.05 if you are single or £189.35 for a couple.

At 65 you can also get the other part of Pension Credit: Savings Credit. That is paid as well as the Guarantee Credit if your weekly income (before Guarantee Credit) is above £91.20 or £145.80 for a couple. You cannot get savings credit if your weekly income is higher than £173.33 (single) or £254.68 (couple).

If you get Guarantee Credit all your Council Tax will be paid, as will a large proportion – sometimes all – of your rent. If you get Savings Credit you may get some or all of your Council Tax and rent paid.

Savings over £6,000 are counted as they are for Council Tax Benefit, but there is no upper limit of £16,000.

You claim pension credit by calling the Pension Credit helpline on 0800 99 1234 (0808 100 6165 in Northern Ireland).You can claim Council Tax Benefit and Housing Benefit at the same time.

You can find out more about Council Tax Benefit, Housing Benefit, and Pension Credit from the Help the Aged leaflet *Can You Claim It?* (see chapter 14).

An alternative is to use the excellent online calculator that works out if you are entitled to any means-tested benefits. It is at www.entitledto.com.

STATE PENSION

You get a **state retirement pension** if you have worked and paid National Insurance contributions for a certain number of years.The rules change from 6 April 2010 and are complicated on each side of that divide.

If you reach pension age before 6 April 2010 (men born 5 April 1945 and *earlier*, women born 5 April 1950 and *earlier*) the old rules apply.

Old rules You need to have at least 44 years (man) or 39 years (woman) of National Insurance contributions to get a full pension, which can be paid at 65 (men) or 60 (women). If you have fewer years than that you get a reduced pension – for example, after 20 years you get 20/44ths of the full pension if you are a man and 20/39ths if you are a woman. But if you have fewer than 11 years (man) or 10 years (woman) you get no pension. Contributions are paid at work or voluntarily and can be credited if you get certain benefits such as Jobseeker's Allowance, Carer's Allowance or some disability benefit.The five years from 60 to 64 are credited anyway (sorry, ladies, men only). People, mainly women, who get Child Benefit or care for another adult also get help called Home Responsibilities Protection towards qualifying for the state pension. Each whole tax year from 1978/9 spent caring reduces the number of years to qualify for a full pension by one. Married women paying the special Married Woman's Contributions often discover too late that those contributions do not count towards a pension *at all*.

That could, possibly, be the first time anyone has ever explained the state pension in less than 200 words, but sadly this will apply only until 5 April 2010.

If you reach pension age on **6 April 2010 or later** (men born 6 **April 1945 or later**; women born 6 **April 1950 or later**), new rules apply.

New rules Pension age for women will rise from 6 April 2010, to 65 from 6 April 2020, and again for everyone from 6 April 2024; eventually pension age will be 68. You need to have at least 30 years (men and women) of National Insurance contributions to get a full pension. If you have less than that you get a reduced pension – for example, after 20 years you get 20/30ths of the full pension. Even if you have as little as one year you get 1/30th. Contributions are paid at work or voluntarily and can be credited if you get certain benefits, such as Child Benefit, Jobseeker's Allowance, Carer's Allowance, or some disability benefits. Some carers who do not get benefits will also get credits. Years of Home Responsibilities Protection will be converted to years of credits. The years from women's pension age to 65 are currently credited to men but will not be after 5 April 2020. Once again, married women paying the special Married Woman's Contributions should note that those contributions do not count towards a pension *at all.*

Those are the new rules in a nutshell. The table opposite shows how to find your pension age.

CLIFF EDGE: WOMEN BORN IN 1950

At the end of 2007 the Government decided to do nothing about the major unfairness which means that a woman born on 6 April 1950 will need 30 years to get a full pension while her neighbour born a day earlier will need 39 years. If they both have 20 years' contributions Ms Later will get about two-thirds of the full pension but Ms Early will get a pension of about half the full amount, about £13 a week less than Ms Later. Parliament may well force the government to think again.

STATE PENSION AGE FOR MEN AND WOMEN

Born	State pension age	State pension age**
Women only *(men's pension age = 65 until 5 April 2020)*		
Up to 5 April 1950	60	60th birthday up to 5 April 2010
6 April 1950 to 5 April 1951	60–61	Between 6 May 2010 and 6 March 2012*
6 April 1951 to 5 April 1952	61–62	Between 6 May 2012 and 6 March 2014*
6 April 1952 to 5 April 1953	62–63	Between 6 May 2014 and 6 March 2016*
6 April 1953 to 5 April 1954	63–64	Between 6 May 2016 and 6 March 2018*
6 April 1954 to 5 April 1955	64–65	Between 6 May 2018 and 6 March 2020*
Men and women		
6 April 1955 to 5 April 1959	65	65th birthday between 6 April 2020 and 5 April 2024
6 April 1959 to 5 April 1960	65–66	Between 6 May 2024 and 6 March 2026*
6 April 1960 to 5 April 1968	66	66th birthday between 6 April 2026 and 5 April 2034
6 April 1968 to 5 April 1969	66–67	Between 6 May 2034 and 6 March 2036*
6 April 1969 to 5 April 1977	67	67th birthday between 6 April 2036 and 5 April 2044
6 April 1977 to 5 April 1978	67–68	Between 6 May 2044 and 6 March 2046*
6 April 1978 and later	68	68th birthday on 6 April 2046 or later

* During the transition periods state pension age is reached on the 6th of odd-numbered months.
** The pension is actually paid from the first Monday on or after state pension age
For your own state pension age enter your date of birth at
www.thepensionservice.gov.uk/resourcecentre/statepensioncalc.asp

MARRIED WOMEN AND CIVIL PARTNERS

The state pension you earn by paying your own contributions is formally called a Category A pension. There is no such thing as a married couple's state pension. But there is a married woman's pension (formally called a Category B pension), which is about 60 per cent of the full Category A pension and is paid to married women on their husband's contributions. A married woman can only get it if her entitlement to a Category A pension on her own contributions is less than the Category B pension she could get on her husband's contributions. For people retiring from 6 April 2010 this pension will also be available to a husband on his wife's contributions and to a civil partner on the other partner's contributions.

There is also a 'dependant's addition' to the state pension which married men can get for a dependent wife under the age of 60. It normally becomes a Category B pension, when she reaches 60 and her husband claims his pension. It is the same amount as a Category B pension and is paid to the husband. No new claims for dependant's addition will be allowed from 6 April 2010 and it will be phased out by 6 April 2020.

EXTRA STATE PENSION

As well as the basic state pension most people get some extra bits and pieces which can be paid even if the state pension is zero. Many women who get no state pension do not realise they can get these extras. They are:

- **Graduated Retirement Benefit** (also called graduated pension), based on National Insurance contributions paid at work from April 1961 to 1975, is a fairly small amount – a few pounds a week at most. Graduated Retirement Benefit will be combined with additional pension from 6 April 2020.
- **additional pension**, also called SERPS (State Earnings-Related Pension Scheme) (6 April 1978 to 5 April 2002) or State Second Pension (S2P) (from 6 April 2002), paid on full National Insurance contributions. People paying into a

pension at work or a personal pension may pay smaller National Insurance contributions which do not count for additional pension. They are called 'contracted-out' contributions. Even people who paid those can get some SERPS. Additional pension can be more than £140 a week but is normally far less – a few tens of pounds in many cases – and will decline to a flat-rate amount in future years.

PENSION-RELATED ISSUES TO THINK ABOUT

How much will I get?
You can get a forecast of your state pension from the Pension Service at www.thepensionservice.gov.uk/resourcecentre/e-services/home.asp but until the autumn of 2008 only those who retire before 6 April 2010 can use this service. The computers are being updated to cope with the new rules.

Deferring pension
You do not have to claim the state pension from your state pension age. If you delay claiming your pension it will be increased by 1 per cent for each five weeks you defer it. So one year's deferral will earn you an extra 10.4 per cent and five years an extra 52 per cent. You can defer as long as you like. Instead of getting extra pension each week you can get the pension you have not claimed paid as a lump sum with generous interest added. After five years that can amount to £30,000 or more. For details see www.thepensionservice.gov.uk/state-pensiondeferral/choices.asp

Married women
More than 300,000 women in their 60s might be able to get a better state pension than they currently have and tens of thousands in their late 50s might be able to enhance the pension they will get. These women have not paid enough National Insurance contributions to get a full pension, often because they were caring for children or a disabled adult.

Two things can go wrong. First, the time they spent caring is not properly recorded on the National Insurance computer. That can happen if they paid the reduced Married Woman's Contributions before they started looking after their children. After two whole tax years not working they should be registered for Home Responsibilities Protection (see brief guide on pages 43–4). But that often did not happen. Only years from April 1978 count for Home Responsibilities Protection. The DWP is supposed to be trawling through records to find these women. Second, women may be able to pay missing contributions back to 1996/7. You cannot pay these contributions if you were working and paying the reduced Married Woman's Contributions and for two whole tax years afterwards, and women cannot pay contributions in the year they reach 60 or subsequent years. The time limit on paying back contributions will be shortened to six years for some people from 6 April 2009 and for everyone from 6 April 2010.

Because this is all so complex even the DWP gets it wrong. So the general rule is that if you are a married woman with an incomplete National Insurance record ask, ask, and ask again whether you can pay extra contributions to fill part of the gap and boost your state pension.

TAX CREDITS

The complexities of means-tested benefits now extend to some new kids on the block known as tax credits. They are mainly for people with children, but they can also be claimed by people in low-paid work without children. Also, if you are 50 or more and returning to employment after a spell out of work the rules are fractionally more generous.

Tax credits are based on a great idea. If you earn a lot you pay tax; if you earn relatively little the tax system gives you some back. When it was just a gleam in the eye of a few academics it was called 'negative income tax' but when it was brought kicking and screaming into a sceptical world in 2001 by Chancellor Gordon Brown it was dubbed 'tax credits'.

This book will not inflict on its readers the details of the calculation needed to work out tax credits. Suffice it to say that the number '37' comes into it quite a lot. Instead, a useful table (page 50) will help you to see if you might qualify. But first, a bit of explanation.

Tax credits help two groups of people:

- Child Tax Credit is for parents and others who bring up children
- Working Tax Credit is for people in low-paid work, whether they have children or not. People over 50 can get a higher rate than younger people when they return to work.

Tax credits can include extra money to help with the costs of childcare. But just to confuse everyone, that is paid as part of Working Tax Credit not with Child Tax Credit.

PEOPLE WHO WORK

Working Tax Credit is paid to people in low-paid work – or who are self-employed with low profits – whether they have children or not. To get it you must normally work for at least 30 hours a week. But people who are disabled or who have children only have to work for 16 hours a week. People aged 50 or more who have just returned to work after at least six months on Jobseeker's Allowance, Income Support or a disability benefit can get a higher rate of Working Tax Credit for the first year and they need only work for 16 hours a week or more. Working Tax Credit is higher for couples and lone parents and for people who are more severely disabled.

Working Tax Credit can be paid at any age. So even if you are over pension age and do some work, you may be able to claim it. However, at that age your state retirement pension – and any other pension – will be added to your wages before the calculation is done and may well mean you do not qualify.

If you work for the minimum wage for 30 hours a week you will earn £8,611 in a year. If you are under 50 and have no children or partner, Working Tax Credit will top up those wages by just over £32 a week or about £1 an hour. If you are single and qualify for the over-50 return-to-work rate you will get £67 a week for the first year. If

WORKING TAX CREDIT 2008/9 – MAXIMUM ANNUAL INCOME (no children)

Basic	16–29 hours**	£10,976
Basic	30+ hours	£12,867
Aged 50 or more*	16–29 hours**	£14,149
Aged 50 or more*	30+ hours	£17,593
Disabled	16–29 hours	£17,144
Disabled	30+ hours	£19,034
Disabled aged 50 or more*	16–29 hours	£20,316
Disabled aged 50 or more*	30+ hours	£23,761

* For one year only on return to work after six months and subject to conditions.

** Must have children

At these income levels you will get the minimum Working Tax Credit of 50p a week.

you have a partner (with no income) the Credit will be £66, so Working Tax Credit is well worth claiming.

The table shows the maximum annual income you can have and get the minimum Working Tax Credit – in other words, if your income is at that level or less some Working Tax Credit will be paid.

PEOPLE WITH CHILDREN

When you add children into the equation things get more complex. **Child Tax Credit** can be paid even if you do not get Working Tax Credit and even if you do not work. It comes in two parts:

- **basic tax credit** – called the 'family element', which is paid to just about everyone with a child and which is £545 a year or about £10.50 a week. However, once your income reaches £50,000 a year the family element is reduced and it disappears once income reaches £57,818. The family element is the same however many children you have but it is doubled in the year a baby is born.

■ **means-tested top-up** – called the 'child element', which is
paid to people with lower incomes – though sometimes
these can be quite high. The full child element is £2,085 a
year for each child but to get that your income has to be
less than £15,575. As your income rises above that the child
element reduces and disappears when income reaches
£19,745. With two children you can still get some child
element with an income below £24,995. Those incomes
are higher if you get Working Tax Credit as well.

Yet a third element is paid with Working Tax Credit: a contribution towards childcare costs. Broadly speaking, if you have children
and pay for childcare it can be worth up to £240 a week and can be
paid to some parents on pretty high incomes – up to £50,000 in
some cases.

Child Tax Credit is for any adult who has the care and responsibility for a child. So if a child lives with a grandparent or other relative
they can claim it even though they are not its parents.

The calculation of tax credits is based on your income – joint
income for a couple who are married or who live as husband and
wife. Income includes all pensions as well as the actual interest earned
on your savings or investments. The capital value of savings does not
count at all. The income is 'gross', that is, before tax or other deductions. But – and it is a huge 'but' – the tax credit is calculated on the
income in a previous tax year. Once awarded, the amount will not normally change for a year. If your income goes down you can tell HM
Revenue and the credit may be increased. But if your income goes up
there is no need to tell the Revenue unless it rises by more than
£25,000. You must also inform the Revenue at once if your personal
circumstances change – for example, the number of children you
have or who you live with.

As the credit is worked out based on income from a previous year,
it will be corrected the following year. So the amount paid will always
be wrong. If it is too much you will get a lot less next year as the over-

payment is recovered. So do not expect it to be simple or straightforward: it is not unusual for people to have problems with this system.

If you get into difficulties, ask for help from the local Citizens Advice office or an advice agency.

Tax credits are claimed from HM Revenue & Customs (tel: 0845 300 3900, or 0845 603 2000 in Northern Ireland to ask for a claim pack). You can check whether you are entitled at the independent website www.entitledto.com and the HMRC website has a lot of information at www.hmrc.gov.uk/menus/credits.htm. At the time of writing you cannot claim online, though that situation may change in 2008.

If you have responsibility for children, remember that you can get Child Benefit, which is £18.80 for the first child and £12.55 for each other child. This too is claimed from HMRC. Child Benefit is not means-tested and every parent should get it.

WINTER FUEL

A really simple benefit, **Winter Fuel Payment**, currently £200 per household, is available where at least one person is aged 60 or more; the amount rises to £300 per household if at least one person is aged 80 or more. The age is calculated at 21 September 2008. The payment is tax-free and does not count as capital when you work out means-tested benefits. Normally the Payment does not have to be claimed because the Department for Work and Pensions knows about you and your age. But if you reach 60 and do not claim a state pension – which is of course mainly men – you should let the DWP know you are entitled. Call the helpline on 08459 15 15 15. For more information see www.thepensionservice.gov.uk/winterfuel/home.asp

DISABILITY AND CARING

As we get older things that worked in our body, things we took for granted, sometimes pack up – or work less well than they should. To some degree it happens to all of us eventually and most people just shrug and say, 'I'm getting old'. But many conditions that we put up with are in fact disabilities. If they get bad enough we can get financial help from the state.

Incapacity Benefit is currently paid to people who are too ill to work and do not get statutory sick pay. It is paid at three rates: £63.75 for the first six months off work, £75.40 for the next six months, and £84.50 for any time after that. It is reduced if you get a company or personal pension of more than £85 a week. From October 2008 Incapacity Benefit is being replaced for new claimants by a new benefit called Employment and Support Allowance, which is less money and has stricter conditions of entitlement. Final details of the new allowance are still being settled as we go to press.

If you have a more severe disability and you need help from someone else with your daily life you may be able to get **Disability Living Allowance** (DLA). That gives you extra money to help with the costs of your personal care and getting around. You have to be under 65 when you claim it. A similar, but more limited, benefit called **Attendance Allowance** is available if you are 65 or more when you first claim.

DLA is paid in two separate parts and there are different rates for each part.

Care component is paid if you need help from someone else to cope with your personal care and the daily tasks of living. You do not have to be actually getting help from anyone already. What is important is that you need help. You must normally have needed this help for the three months immediately before you claim and you must expect to need help for the six months afterwards.

There are three rates of care component, depending on how much help you need from someone else:

- highest rate – £67.00 per week
- middle rate – £44.85 per week
- lowest rate – £17.75 per week.

The definitions are complex and often changed in subtle ways after court decisions about what exactly they mean. But broadly speaking, for the lowest rate you must need attention from another person to deal with some 'bodily function' for more than an hour a day. Or you must be unable to cook a main meal for yourself if you have the ingredients. It does not matter whether you actually cook or not. What counts is whether you could carry out all the activity involved in cooking such as using a knife, a cooker and taps.

To qualify for the middle or highest rate you must need frequent attention from someone else and the rules about what that means are different depending whether you need it during the day or the night.

To qualify by day you must need frequent attention from someone else with your bodily functions 'throughout the day'. Although that includes the middle of the day as well as the morning or evening it does not have to be all day or even every day. Your bodily functions are things like eating, preparing meals, using the toilet, getting up, washing and dressing, taking medication or using a wheelchair. It also means walking and other physical activities that allow you to carry out a reasonable level of social, recreational or leisure activity. Blind or deaf people who need help with daily tasks because of their lack of sight or hearing may also qualify. You may qualify if you have a condition such as epilepsy where someone has to be around to avoid you putting yourself in danger, even if that may happen only occasionally.

To qualify by night you must need attention more than once and for more than 20 minutes at a time in connection with your bodily functions. Or someone has to be around for a prolonged period or at frequent intervals for the purpose of watching over you to avoid substantial danger to yourself or others.

If you qualify by day or night you get the middle rate. If you qualify for both you get the highest rate.

Mobility component is paid if you have difficulty in walking or getting around. There are two rates. You must normally have had mobility problems for the three months immediately before you claim and expect to have the same difficulties for the six months afterwards.

- Higher rate is £46.75
- Lower rate is £17.75

To qualify for the higher rate, you must be unable to walk, or have great difficulty walking, or be in serious danger if you do walk. You may also get it if you can walk but only with great pain, or can only walk a short distance or at a slow pace.

You may qualify for the lower rate of mobility component even if you can walk. But you must need guidance or supervision from someone else to make sure you are safe or to help you find your way around in a strange place.

An organisation called Motability helps people use the highest rate of mobility component to purchase or lease a vehicle. However, your benefit may not cover all the costs; you may have to pay a deposit or for the cost of adaptations and you will have to pay the running costs. Do check exactly what you will need to pay before committing yourself.

Both components of DLA are tax-free and paid on top of other benefits and pensions. In fact, once you qualify some rates of means-tested benefit go up.

If you claim DLA it can continue to any age. But you cannot claim it for the first time once you are 65. Instead, you claim Attendance Allowance – a cut-down version of DLA that does not include the lower rate of care component, or any mobility allowance.

CARERS

There are about 6 million unpaid carers in the UK. If these unpaid carers did not do this work it would cost taxpayers an estimated £57 billion, i.e. £57,000,000,000, a year. Many people become carers in their 50s but research shows that about one in four over-50s simply do not know that they can get any financial help for doing that important job.

In truth, the financial help you can get is pretty pathetic. **Carer's Allowance** is only £50.55 a week – just over £2,600 a year – worth having, but not enough to live on. To get it you have to care for at least 35 hours a week – which works out at just £1.44 an hour (so much for the minimum wage!). And of course most carers spend far more time than that looking after the other person. If you care for 100 hours a week it works out at 50p an hour.

But there are two other advantages of getting Carer's Allowance. First, as long as you tell the DWP you will get a credit towards your National Insurance contributions. Second, you can also claim Income Support without worrying about looking for work.

If you do work your Carer's Allowance stops if you earn more than £95 a week – about 17 hours' work on the minimum wage. If you do work and care you are entitled to 'reasonable' time off to help the person you care for.

In order to claim Carer's Allowance it is not enough to be looking after someone else. The person cared for has to be getting either Attendance Allowance or Disability Living Allowance at the middle or highest rate. The lowest rate does not count and neither does the mobility component.

If you get state pension you cannot get Carer's Allowance as well – they are said to 'overlap'. But it is still worth claiming because it gives you what is called an 'underlying entitlement' to Carer's Allowance and that can boost the amount of Pension Credit and other means-tested benefits that you get.

If you are a carer your local council has an obligation to assess your needs but it does not have to meet those needs if it cannot afford to do so.

You can find out more from Carers UK on 0808 808 7777 or at www.carersuk.org.

This chapter is not a full guide to benefits. It is a snapshot of what is available. One thing we do know about all benefits is that not everyone who can get them does. And that is particularly true of means-tested benefits and those for disability and caring.

So it is always worth asking for help from one of the organisations that can advise you. A good place to start is the Help the Aged SeniorLine freephone advice service (see chapter 14). ■

4
SAVING

SAVING

Saving and investing are about making your money work harder so you don't have to. Before anyone even thinks about saving or investing – and why they are different and which they should do – there is one key question to ask: **do you have debts?**

If the answer is 'yes', you must, before you even think about putting a penny into a savings account or an investment, **pay off your debts**.

The one exception might be – only *might* be – your mortgage (see pages 175–9). But if you have a credit card that you do not pay off in full each month, an overdraft, a personal loan, debts on catalogue purchases or any other debt at all, don't save and don't invest.

Here's why. The average interest charged on a credit card debt or overdrafts is about 16 per cent. The average paid out on savings is about 3 per cent. The difference is 13 per cent. So if you have £1,000 worth of debt it will cost you about £160 a year just to pay the interest due. At the end of the year you will have spent £160 and still owe £1,000. If you have another £1,000 in a savings account, even if it earns 3 per cent, you will get back £30 less £6 tax so that means you end up with £24 (and a nice warm glow, of course, knowing that you have given the government a tenner). Knock that £24 off your £160 cost and you have spent £136.

AUTHOR'S CONFESSION

When I was first self-employed I carefully put a third of everything I earned into a separate savings account so I knew it was there to pay my tax at the end of the year. I did that even though it meant sometimes my current account went overdrawn (I had an overdraft arrangement, of course, which kept down the cost of going overdrawn). But even if I was overdrawn I knew I had the money to pay my tax. I knew it cost me over the year. But I called that expense my 'sleep at night' money. So like all rules, the one about not saving if you have debt can be broken for a good reason.

But if you use your £1,000 to pay off your debt you spend nothing during the year – saving £136. So before you save, pay off debt.

If you have debts, turn now to chapter 9, which tells you about good debt and bad debt, how the banks make money out of you, and how to pay debts off. If you do not have debts, carry on with this chapter and see how to make your money work for you as hard as you worked for it in the first place.

SAVE OR INVEST?

So you have no debts. You have some money to spare. You want it to earn money.

First, understand that saving and investing are different – very different. But they are often confused, even by the government. The Treasury confuses them by using calling its tax-free deal an 'individual savings account' or ISA. Some ISAs are savings accounts. But many others are in fact investments. National Savings & Investments – which should surely know as it has both words in its name – uses the terms interchangeably. It calls its 'passbook savings account' an investment account and says its savings certificates offer a 'range of investment terms'. But the difference is vital.

If you save, your money remains yours. If you invest, your money belongs to someone else. It is that simple – and that important.

Here is how the difference works. Let us assume that you have £1,000 to spare. You go online and open a savings account. You transfer the money into it. The £1,000 remains yours. You have lent it to the online bank. A year later, you need the money back. You go online and transfer the money back to your current account, visit a cash machine and take it out. And the bank has added £50. It takes off £10 tax which leaves you with a **profit** of £40 – for no work. Magic!

For the whole year that money was yours and it was not at risk. You could always get it back.

Alternatively, let us imagine that you have heard that wine is a very good investment. So you go along to a wine merchant and speak to Justin Oenophile, who recommends a case of 12 bottles of a fine Bordeaux, from a chateau called Bonterroir. It costs £1,000, which works out at more than £80 a bottle. But you have heard that the price of fine wine has doubled in the last year or so. You take the wine home and put it in the cellar, or more likely the cupboard under the stairs. A year later, you need the money back. You have resisted drinking even one bottle of the Bonterroir but you cannot take the wine to the bank and cash it in. You have to sell it. But when you go back to Mr Oenophile, who warmly recommended that particular chateau, told you how well it had done and said that if he was investing in one case of wine that would be his choice, he now says that for some reason there is a bit of a glut of wine from that particular part of Bordeaux ('It's left bank, you know, and right bank is much more in demand this year'). Eventually, muttering something about grape varieties and soil conditions, he reluctantly offers you a take-it-or-leave-it £450 – and that is cutting his own throat. **Loss: £550.**

That is the difference between saving and investing. And just because most investments involve money rather than wine that does not mean that the money you use to buy them is still yours. It is not. Just as when you buy wine, the money becomes someone else's. The investment is yours. To get your money back depends on their honesty when they sell you the investment, and whether someone – anyone! – will want to buy it when you want to sell it – and at what price.

So if you have money to spare or you want something in the future and you are 'saving up' for it, should you save or invest? The answer you will get from most financial advisers is 'How much you are prepared to risk?'. Often they use the word 'appetite', as in 'your risk appetite', or even ask you 'What is your appetite for risk?'. Most people have not got a clue, nor do they really understand what is being asked. In fact most financial advisers do not fully understand risk.

Risk will be further discussed later, but for now it is the wrong question. When you consider whether to save or invest the only question you should ask yourself is 'When will I need this money?'. If the answer is within one year, you should save. If it is in 40 years' time, you should invest. If it is somewhere in between, it depends. Up to about five years, saving is always the answer, and even up to ten it can be the right thing to do. Over that and you might think of investing.

That is where the difficult choices begin.

SAVING ESSENTIALS

Saving should be simple. You lend your money to the bank or building society, it pays you for the loan by adding a certain percentage to the money you lent. It is like rent for using your money and it can be paid every month or every year or, sometimes, when you take back the money you have lent it.

Because interest is expressed simply as a percentage, comparing one savings deal with another should be easy. Interest at 4.5 per cent should always be better than interest at 3.9 per cent but worse than interest at 5.6 per cent (if you are saving, of course: if you are borrowing the opposite is true). And so it used to be. But over the last 20 years the banks have tried out every means they can devise to make it complicated, difficult and confusing – 'complexification', we might call it. Others have described it in shorter and less sympathetic terms – 'deceit' being about the simplest.

It sometimes seems as if the banks have teams of people devoted to working out ways to take money off us in such a way that we will not really notice. Some of the cleverest tricks are reserved for when they lend us money. But they are pretty sharp when it comes to borrowing money off us – in other words, persuading us to deposit our money with them.

Generally it is better to ignore all the trickery and go for a simple, instant access, cash savings account that offers the best rate of interest. Now let's look at what all those words mean, starting at the end.

Interest rate This is the rent the bank pays you for the use of your money. If you lend it £1,000 and the interest is 5 per cent then you should get £50 back for each year they have it. Ah, if only it were that

AER AND GROSS INTEREST

Interest can be paid monthly or annually or sometimes at the end of the deal when you take your money back. Let's say you put £1,000 in a bank account and the interest is paid monthly. Say the gross rate is 6 per cent but it is paid monthly at 0.5 per cent (6 per cent/12 = 0.5 per cent). So each month 0.5 per cent is added on to your £1,000.

At the end of month 1, you have £1,005. In month 2 that £1005 is earning interest, so at the end of month 2 you will earn not £5 interest but £5.03. That is because the £5 is also earning interest. By the end of month 12 you have earned £61.68 instead of the £60 that 6 per cent on £1,000 might imply. The AER rate is therefore not 6 per cent but 6.168 per cent, which is always rounded to two decimal places so it will be expressed as 6.17 per cent.

This is because, over the year, the money you invested (the £1,000) has earned £61.68. Now that bonus of £1.68 may not seem very much. But if you let it run another year instead of £120 you will have earned £127.16. And after five years you will have earned £348.85 instead of £300. So where interest is paid more frequently than annually, AER is higher than gross.

simple! Interest on savings can be quoted gross or using something called AER (which stands for Annual Equivalent Rate: in other words the rate your money would earn if you left it in for a year). When making comparisons, always look at the AER because you can be (fairly) sure that the one that is bigger is the one that is better.

The box above explains the difference between AER and gross interest. Skip it if you do not need (or want) to know.

As you have realised, AER and gross are the same when the interest is paid annually. Accordingly, of course, where the interest is paid less frequently than every year AER is less than gross. For example, if your £1,000 earns £60 a year but it is not paid until the end of two years (so £120 is added to your money), then it still 6 per cent gross but is 5.68 per cent AER. And if you let it run five years and it earned just £300, still 6 per cent gross, but just 5.26 per cent AER.

That is why it is important only to compare AERs and why the law says the AER must be shown as the most prominent figure. So the important thing to check is the AER. If company A offers a rate of 5.89 per cent gross and company B offers 5.95 per cent gross, which pays the better interest? You might think it was company B as its interest rate is higher. But no. Company A pays interest monthly but company B only pays it annually. So company B has an AER of 5.95 per cent but company A has an AER of 6.05 per cent. So if you leave the money invested company A pays the better rate.

BEST BUYS

So, with one number to look out for – AER – it should be easy to compare savings accounts. You can do that easily by logging on to one of the many comparison sites on the internet or looking in a 'best buy' table in the paper. But sadly, it is not that easy. Best buy tables are a blessing and a curse. There are three problems with them.

First, none of them has data on every single savings account (or every single one of anything – this is a general problem of these tables, not just a savings account problem). There are various reasons for this.

The sites generally charge companies to be featured (they dress this charge up in many ways, such as calling it a 'subscription' to their services, but basically it is a charge). However, some smaller companies – especially building societies and credit unions – cannot afford the fee, which can run to tens of thousands of pounds a year. Some companies just choose to opt out of the tables. And others can be excluded. For two years one foreign-owned bank which operated in the UK did not appear simply because it did not subscribe to the Banking Code. Once it did, the bank and its very good savings offers appeared in the comparison sites.

Secondly, because the best buy lists are businesses and want to make money they offer special deals to some customers in exchange for a fee. That is why you will see a series of 'sponsored links' above a best buy list. They are *not* the best buys – they have just paid to be there. So always look down the page to where the genuine best buys begin. As ever, the AER is the clue.

The third problem with best buy tables is more subtle. Banks and building societies add bells and whistles to push their product up towards the top of the table. On savings accounts many offer a 'bonus' which is a higher rate of interest for six or 12 months so that the AER appears very good. But in fact at the end of that period the rate is rubbish. For example, at the time of writing six of the top 15 instant access savings accounts have a bonus for a period ranging from six months to a year. One building society offers 6 per cent, putting it in the top three, but after a year that rate plummets to 5 per cent, which would take it down to 56th place. So unless you remember to move your money after a year you will stop getting a decent return – and clearly, a lot of people do just that. They let their money languish in accounts that may once have been good but are now rubbish: one of today's examples pays just 1.11 per cent. Even that is not the worst. Some pay 0.25 per cent a year.

Not everyone agrees that AER is the thing to use. For example, MoneyFacts, the oldest comparison service, always quotes rates gross. It does that because some people do not leave their money invested. They want interest paid monthly because they use it to boost their income. In the above example, company B would be ahead of company A in Moneyfacts' best buys because it has the higher gross rate. But it would be the other way round in some other best buy tables. For example, fool.co.uk ranks savings accounts according to AER but it gives both AER and gross rates.

CHANGING RATES AND OTHER PITFALLS

Whichever measure you use, rule number one of cash savings is – watch the rate (it will change). The Dutch bank ING burst on the UK

savings scene in 2003 offering a market-leading rate. But now it lan-
guishes in the bottom half of the top 100, having decided not to pass
on three rate rises to its customers. Many voted with their feet – there
were reports that £3 billion was moved to its competitors. That is
one kind of stampede to follow.

Rates change so frequently that every example in this book should
be treated as just that – an example, and like any information or advice
to do with the financial world, it goes out of date quickly.

There are less obvious traps, too. One is the withdrawal fine. For
example, Halifax offers an apparently OK rate of 5.5 per cent on its
guaranteed saver account as long as you invest at least £5,000. But if
you make more than four withdrawals of money in the year you lose
30 days' interest. That would slash the rate to little more than 5 per
cent. Some fine you for one withdrawal, others for more than a certain number. Always avoid them.

Another is the 'regular saver account'. Some of these offer mad
rates – one recently offered was as high as 12 per cent. But these
accounts only last a year, then dump your money into a rubbish account
at the end of it, while you have to commit yourself to paying a fixed
amount in each month – and nothing more. So in fact you will end
up with about half the advertised rate on the total amount you put in.

Other tricks are to encourage you to open a linked current
account – which may be not very good – and some building societies
allow only local people to get the best deals.

So the way to get the most on your savings is:

■ go to several 'best buy' sites
■ tick the boxes to get instant access and no bonus rates
  (and then monthly or annual interest, depending which
  you want)
■ pick the best AER for the amount you have to save.

Remember, these accounts pay a variable rate of interest. That
means the bank can put the rate up or down as it chooses. Usually

it will happen when the Bank of England and its grandly named Monetary Policy Committee decide to change the official bank rate. So after a year check what rate you are getting. If it is not the best, move your money. Banks show no loyalty to us. We should show none to them.

FIXED-TERM ACCOUNTS

There is one way in which a bit of loyalty, or at least commitment, can pay a small bonus. Instant access is fine. But if you do have money that you absolutely, completely, 100 per cent know that you will not need for a period of time you can earn a bit more and, unlike instant access accounts, the rate is guaranteed; unlike instant accounts you of course have no instant access to your money. These are called fixed-term accounts or sometimes bonds (however, bonds can mean many, many things, some of them not in the least desirable, so do not assume that they are a Good Thing). The deal is this: you deposit your cash and promise not to take it back for, say, a year and the bank or building society gives you a guaranteed fixed rate.

Two things push up the rate you might get over an instant access account:
1 the bank knows it has your money for a fixed term and can use that money for its own fixed-term deals in loans and mortgages
2 to do those deals the banks need money and, at the moment, banks trust us more than they trust each other. So your cash attracts a premium rate

But fixed-term deals are a gamble. You are betting on whether interest rates will rise or fall during the time your money is tied up. If they go down you win the bet. If they go up you lose and – guess what? – the bank wins. Fixed-term savings accounts require a serious amount of money – at least £1,000 (the usual minimum) – to take them up. As ever, look at the AER to decide which is best.

CURRENT ACCOUNTS

You may not keep much in your current account – or indeed it may have a minus sign in front of it (see pages 145–71 for more on debt) – but however little is in there, it should be working. Nowadays you can get a reasonable rate of interest on your current account too.

Generally the high street banks pay a derisory 0.1 per cent interest on standard current accounts – though a couple of them pay nothing. That means you are lending the bank the money for nothing. Suppose your balance on average over the year is £100. If you got 5 per cent paid on that (which is possible), at the end of the year your money would have earned you a fiver.

Not much, you may say. But if you saw one lying in the street, would you pick it up? Or, if that makes you feel uncomfortable ('Yes, but I'd take it to the police station'), put it another way. Do you have a fiver in your pocket or purse now? Take it out. Hold it up. And tear it in half. Not so easy is it? Letting the bank keep a fiver we could get on our money is just the same as tearing up a fiver you already have. We are a nation which waits for 1p change at the shop but happily lets the banks take pounds off us not so much without bothering about it, more without even noticing.

Just think what is happening to your money. While the bank is paying you 0.1 per cent (and on £100 that is just 10p interest over the year) it is using it, lending it out, doing deals – in other words, making your money – *your money* – work for it. Over the year that £100 might earn the bank anything up to £15, while you get 10p. It is a scandal.

Lecture over. Now, what about good current accounts?

CHOOSING THE ACCOUNT THAT WORKS FOR YOU

The first question is, how will you use your account? If you will go overdrawn occasionally or even often (but not all the time because you agreed at the start of this chapter to pay it off: if you have debt there is little point in reading the next bit until you have done that), you need to find an account which offers the best deal on overdrafts.

If that is you, turn to page 159 where debt and overdrafts are discussed.

So, goody-two-shoes, you do not go overdrawn and you want to find the best current account. Once again, it all comes down to AER. Some, the big high street banks, pay 0.1 per cent – or even nothing. But others pay you a decent rate – 3 or 4 per cent. You can get more, but that usually comes with strings attached, and in banking and financial services strings are generally not good.

Here are some of the strings you will find.

'The first slice is the biggest' Under this scheme, you get a better rate on a certain amount but nothing (or maybe 0.1 per cent) on amounts above that. The idea is to stop you using your current account as a savings account. What's wrong with that? No one knows, but the banks don't like it.

The monthly fee Some banks charge you for running a current account. The bank spins the fee to say it is to pay for exciting stuff such as insurance – which often you do not want and may not need (or *vice versa*). It is never worth it.

Buy another product This gives you a better deal if you open another account or buy an investment or a mortgage. This 'string' is held by the sales department and should never be followed.

Pay in a minimum amount This is the only condition, or string, worth considering. If you pay £500 or £1,000 into your account each month you may get a better rate. If you have that sort of income (and with a joint account that usually means between you), doing this may lead you to a decent higher-interest rate.

There is something else you can do to get a better rate of interest: go online. Many of the better no-strings rates are found with accounts you run through your computer.

ONLINE BANKING

Some people are afraid of doing their banking online. They are afraid of someone stealing their money – or their identity. If surveys are to be believed ID theft is one of our biggest worries. But online banking itself is safe. Yes, there are thieves around the world who will try to get hold of your money. Yes, sometimes they are successful. But you can protect yourself against them quite easily. It is just like closing your windows at night or locking your front door when you go out. To stay safe online you just need to follow a few basic security steps.

First, deal with your bank only through its own website and by logging on in the normal way. If you get an email that claims it is from your bank, delete it unread. Never ever click on a link in an email: it can lead you into trouble. And never put any details of your bank into an email. Unfortunately, it is just possible that your bank might send you an email. Marketing departments like to do that, if only to see the security guys tearing their hair out. But it will never be anything important, so delete it. If you really want to follow it up, log on in the usual way or call the bank (all online banks have a telephone helpline as well).

Even emails that are not from your bank should be treated with care. Never click on an email link or open an attachment with an email unless it is from someone you know and trust (and does not look as if it has just been forwarded). Attachments can contain software that downloads to your computer and steals passwords as you type them in the keyboard.

The other big thing to remember about online banking is that if you do lose money (which is very rare, but of course very upsetting if it happens to be you), the bank will reimburse you – perhaps not as quickly as you would like, but it is the bank, not you, that bears the cost.

For more on ID theft and staying safe online see pages 168–71 below.

OPENING YOUR NEW BANK ACCOUNT

Once you have decided on your new current account – perhaps online and definitely paying a decent rate of interest on your money – you have to change to that new bank. It is very easy to do. Open the new account. Tell the old bank you want it to close your account and transfer any balance to the new account. It will move all the standing orders and direct debits you have coming out of your account: this should all happen within a couple of weeks or so. You will have to tell your employer or pension provider and anyone else who pays money into your current account. And that's it: money working harder.

TAX

Before we move on to other savings products, a word about tax. HM Revenue & Customs likes to take money off us and then wait for us to claim it back if it has taken too much. So it automatically whips off 20p of every pound earned in interest on our savings, even from accounts opened by children. Almost half the population does not pay income tax – just over 30 million of us do, out of a population of about 60 million. The non-taxpayers include almost all children, about one in two pensioners, and many adults who are parents, unemployed, disabled or simply kept by someone else. If you are not a taxpayer but you have some money in a current account or savings account, stop the Revenue taking the tax it has no right to by filling in a form called R85. You can download it from www.hmrc.gov.uk/forms/r85.pdf

If a couple has a joint savings account and one partner does not pay tax, the bank or building society should be willing to pay half the interest tax-free if R85 is filled in. Some are awkward about doing it. If they are, be insistent.

If tax has been wrongly deducted in previous years it can be claimed back for up to six previous tax years. Hence, in 2008/9 it can be claimed back to 2002/3 but not before. You do that using form R40. Note that you will need one R40 for each past tax year. Download the form from www.hmrc.gov.uk/forms/r40.pdf. You can use the same form as long as you put the correct tax year at the top.

Remember that you can reclaim tax not only when no tax has been due but if you are due to pay tax only at the lower 10 per cent rate. That rate is much rarer now (see pages 187–8 for details) but if your income is low you may have a claim to make. Find out more from the taxback helpline 0845 077 6543 or at www.hmrc.co.uk/taxback.

ISAs

If you do not want to pay tax at all, you can put your money in a cash ISA (Individual Savings Account). These are specially registered savings accounts on which no tax is paid by anyone. There are of course limits on how much you can put in. In 2008/9 you can pay in up to £3,600. You can put in any amount from £1 to the maximum each year. You can take money out when you want. But you can only put it back up to the limit. So if you have already put in £3,600 in 2008/9 and you then take out £1,000, you cannot put that back until next year. But if you have only put in £2,600 this year and take out £1,000 you can still put in another £1,000 this year.

Because they are so flexible, cash ISAs are the sensible way for taxpayers to save, even for fairly short-term items like Christmas or a holiday. Anyone who can afford it should put in the full amount each year. More than £120 billion is saved in cash ISAs, saving the owners at least £1 billion a year in tax.

You can move money which is in a cash ISA into another one if the rate is better. So if a better fund comes along you can move your money to get the best rate. If you do want to move your cash from one ISA to another you cannot take it out and put it somewhere else – that would breach the annual limit. You have to open the new ISA – making sure it is one that will take ISA transfers – and then ask the two banks to transfer the money from one to another. That way you keep it in an ISA and preserve its tax-free status.

All these rules on flexibility are what the law allows. The banks and building societies impose their own restrictions, which they are legally entitled to do. For example, many offering the best rate do not let you move money from another ISA so you are confined to putting in the annual amount. Others welcome transferred funds and pay higher rates the bigger the total you have. Some only allow transactions in lumps of £250 or make you open another linked account. Others impose a penalty if you withdraw money without giving them notice. Avoid all this nonsense. Look for the top rate that is paid on an easy-access ISA and put in what you can afford up to the limit. In that way, you can use it as your day-to-day savings account.

OTHER WAYS TO SAVE

So far we have talked about instant-access, no-conditions savings accounts. That is partly because there is one important rule in saving – keep it simple – and partly because we never know what life will throw at us. A deal that ties you in for two years may look great when you take it out but then, if your daughter announces she is getting married, your son wants help with his house deposit, a teenage descendant needs a first car (or, even worse, the money to insure it), you may discover that cancelling the deal costs you so much you might as well have kept your money as used tenners in the biscuit tin.

Savings deals that tie up your money up should therefore be treated with caution. Generally they do not give you the best rates, and when they do give you a good rate the premium for tying up your money over the best instant access is pretty poor. But here is a quick guide to the alternatives which impose restrictions.

NATIONAL SAVINGS
The most cautious of the cautious cannot doubt that National Savings & Investments is safe. That is its big selling point. It is backed by the UK government and, short of nuclear war or revolution, there are no conceivable circumstances in which you will not get back what you put in and the bonus you have been promised. NS&I trades on that to give goodish but not the best rates.

National Savings products also have a choice of tax regimes. Some products pay interest tax-free – in other words, no tax is due on the money your money earns. That is clearly better for taxpayers, and the higher the rate of tax you pay the better it is. Some other products generate interest which is taxable but it is paid gross, before tax is deducted. That means you have the money for longer until you sort out the tax at the end of the year with your self-assessment tax form.

PREMIUM BONDS

If you buy Premium Bonds, you know your capital is safe. But the interest earned is put into a pool and each month each bond has a chance of winning a prize drawn by the famous Ernie – Electronic Random Number Indicator Equipment (don't call him a computer – he's not and is easily insulted).

Prizes range from £50 to £1 million and are tax-free so they are best for higher-rate taxpayers, and you need a lot of bonds to have a good chance of winning regularly. With the maximum £30,000 you can expect 15 prizes a year but almost all of those will be £50. Even with £30,000 worth of bonds you have an even chance of winning a prize of £5,000 or more once every 89 years, and even a prize of £500 or £1,000 only a little more than once every four years. With 100 bonds your chances of winning any prize at all are tiny – just once every 20 years.

NS&I tells us that the rate of interest that goes into the prize pool is 3.8 per cent. But nearly a third of that goes to the bigger prizes, which you are very unlikely to win, so the effective rate is 2.66 per cent. So although Premium Bonds are fun and there is that 17 billion-to-one chance of winning £1 million, they are not a good way of saving unless you are a higher-rate taxpayer and can buy, if not the maximum, at least £10,000 worth, and leave it there a long time.

Premium Bonds are National Savings' most popular product.

Of the other National Savings products only one is really interesting: index-linked bonds guarantee to increase your investment in line with inflation and pay, at the moment, 1.35 per cent on top, all of which is tax-free. The bonds use the RPI measure of inflation, which reached well over 4 per cent in 2007. So the tax-free return of around 5.5 per cent is potentially very good. You can always be sure that your savings will more than keep up with inflation. You have to keep the bond for three or five years.

Other NS&I products usually tie your money up for a period of time and the rates can usually be beaten by other providers.

OTHER SAVINGS PRODUCTS

There are more than 4,000 savings accounts of various sorts. Some will ask you to tie your money up for a year or more, some will offer a fixed rate for that period, others will ask you to pay in a regular amount, and a growing number will offer 'special deals' for people of over 50 or 60. Most of these are best avoided. At the moment the real competition is in instant cash savings and that is where the best rates are. But you must watch your money and move it when that deal turns sour. If you can tie your money up, some of the fixed-rate bonds mentioned earlier are worth considering. ∎

5
INVESTING

INVESTING

I f you have turned directly to this chapter without looking at the start of chapter 4, where the essential differences between saving and investing are explained, turn back and read it now. This book is not about investment. In a way it is about avoiding it. Investment will not boost your income in the short-term. Investment is for the long term – ten years or more – and if you are lucky it can leave you better off. So let's start with some rules.

Never invest if you have debt. You can get away with having a bit of debt and still putting some money into your sleep-at-night cash savings (see page 59). That is understandable psychologically, if not arithmetically. But investing when you have debt is a recipe for ruin. Debt is certain but investment is a gamble. Never mix certain liabilities (debts) and uncertain returns (investments).

Always take good independent financial advice. That sounds easy and at the moment, fortunately, all financial advisers have to tell you whether or not they are independent (if they are not, do not use them). But they do not have to tell you if they are any good (for more on choosing an adviser see pages 96–8).

When you invest money, it is no longer yours. As explained on pages 60–2, when you invest you buy something off someone else. They have your money. You have a piece of paper (unless you have invested in goods, such as the 12 bottles of wine in the earlier example). So when you need your money you have to sell the investment, which means finding a buyer who will pay what you want.

Investment is a gamble. It may pay off and you may do very well. But you may not. As with all gambles, the more you limit your risk the less chance you have of making a lot of money but the less chance you have of losing a lot. The other side of the coin is that the more risk you take there is always a small chance of making a very good return. But there is also a bigger chance of losing money. Sometimes you can lose the lot.

Keep some money in cash. Even if investment is for you, keep some of your spare money in cash so that you can cope with life's little fluctuations.

Keep these rules in mind and you will avoid the worst traps.

WHERE TO INVEST

So you have paid off your debts. You have some cash savings earning a good return. You still have some money left over that you can afford not to spend for a few years, preferably at least ten, and you want to invest it. How do you go about it?

Over the last 50 years one sort of investment has come to dominate all others – the stock market. Most of the money invested by private individuals is ultimately invested in shares of companies. Let's start with the basics. What is a share?

SHARES

A share is simply what it says – a share of a company. Usually it is a very small share –often less than a billionth – but the money you have used to buy those shares is then tied to that company and how much other people are prepared to pay for its shares.

To see how shares work, consider one of Britain's favourite companies, Marks & Spencer. There are about 1.7 billion shares in M&S. So if you have one share you own just under half of one-billionth of the company. At the time of writing each share was worth about £6.30, making the whole company worth 1.7 billion x £6.30 = £10.7 billion.

If you own a share, you can make money in two ways:

1 each year the company will pay you some of the profit it makes. It does that by paying what is called a dividend on each share

2 the value of your share will go up and down but overall you hope the value will rise.

These two ways of making money are quite separate. Usually, people concentrate on the rise in the value of the shares. But the return, the dividends you earn, can also be important.

In 2007 Marks & Spencer made about £936 million in profit. If that profit had been divided equally among the shareholders they would each have received 55p for each share they owned (in fact, it is not that simple as not all profits are counted and the actual profit per share given by M&S is 40p). But shareholders are just one demand on the profits. The company has to invest money for the future (that cost M&S £792 million in 2007), pay off debt, keep some money back for possible bad times ahead, and needs to keep a balance in the bank to support its day-to-day spending. In 2007 M&S gave shareholders just 18.3p for each of their shares. Considering each share was worth £6.30 that represents a return of just under 3 per cent on their money.

Dividends come twice a year in two unequal instalments, and if you own shares in a number of individual companies they can provide a useful income. But the main way people expect to make money out of shares is by the rise in their value. They expect the price of the shares to go up over the period they hold them.

M&S UPS AND DOWNS

In August 2006 you could buy M&S shares for £5.77. A year later they were worth £6.30. So the value of your share grew by 53p in a year – a lot more than the 18.3p dividend. Of course, the value of shares can go down as well as up, and much of that gain was lost over the next few months. Some years ago M&S shares plummeted in value and in 2003/4 were worth barely half their current price. But those who stayed loyal got their reward when shares went back above £7.

WHY SHARES FLUCTUATE IN VALUE

Shares go up and down in price because of the one law of economics that works – supply and demand. When there is a shortage of something – in other words, the demand for it exceeds the supply of it – the price rises. When there is too much of something – in other words, the supply of it is bigger than demand for it – the price falls. It's that simple. The law of supply and demand (which is actually expressed in a slightly more complex way by economists, who have to retain some mystery), is the e = mc² of economics. It is universally and always true, as well as being a lot easier to understand than Einstein's famous equation.

The price of a share in a particular company depends on what makes people want to buy it or sell it. Some of these things make sense. Shares in a company which is making good profits should be more valuable than those of a company that is making a loss. The people who run it are also important. Do the directors do their job well? Have they got a clear vision of the future? And is the business they are in one that is likely to survive?

The price is also affected by things that are nothing to do with the performance of the business at all. If investors believe that the price of shares in a company will rise, they can buy for that reason alone, hoping to make a quick profit. That can happen when there is a rumour or a suspicion that a company may be bought by another. Shares in the target company rise in the belief that the price will go up as the predator tries to persuade shareholders to sell. When the entrepreneur Phillip Green revealed that he wanted to buy Marks & Spencer in May 2004 the price of its shares rose by almost £1 each overnight.

On the other hand, if a rumour spreads that a company is in trouble, investors will sell its shares and the value will fall. Other investors, who may know nothing of the reasons for the fall, will want to get out too before things get worse, so they will also sell, sending the price of the shares into a downward spiral.

Apart from attitudes to individual companies, there are fads. In the late 1990s investors went overboard for hi-tech companies, especially those providing internet-based services. People believed they were the next big thing and the price of their shares could only rise. So they bought them, and as demand grew so did the price. The dot.com bubble, as it is often called, was a good example of irrationality gripping financial markets. A quick look at the accounts and annual reports of almost all the hi-tech companies showed that they lost money every year, had no prospect of making profits, and had huge debts. In March 2000 investors paused for a reality check. Shares in hi-tech companies fell out of favour and the prices plummeted, taking a lot of other companies down too. The market has still not recovered from that crash.

In retrospect we can see what the investors got wrong. Internet companies were the next big thing. But not the ones whose core business was not integral to the internet, such as those selling books or holidays. Eventually it was the search engine Google, the social networking Facebook and the video-clip channel YouTube that suddenly became worth billions of pounds.

In 2007 the market was driven up by what is called 'M&A activity' – mergers and acquisitions. Many wealthy individuals and investment funds were prowling around looking for companies they could buy to make a quick profit. So shares in companies became seen as a good way to make money – the company you own shares in may be the next target. So the whole market is driven higher by nothing more than the thought – the hope – of making money.

Other factors can also affect the price of shares. It generally rises at times of political and economic stability. At other times, particularly when there is political uncertainty, investors move their money out of shares and into other things – such as gold – which are supposed to be less subject to politics.

So the price of shares – either in one company or as a whole – fluctuates day by day, month by month, year by year in a largely unpredictable fashion.

HOW SHARE PRICES ARE REPORTED

Share prices are tracked through the indices you hear quoted on the news bulletins – the FTSE ('Footsie') in London, the Dow in New York, and the Nikkei in Tokyo. You hear about those three out of the thousands of indices there are partly because of time zones – they are about a third of a day apart and therefore cover the whole 24-hour period. As the Nikkei goes to sleep, the FTSE crunches its cornflakes. When the FTSE takes its afternoon nap the Dow in New York grabs a skinny latte on the way to work. And as the bell rings for the end of the Dow's day, the Nikkei is stretching itself over a bowl of noodles. The sun never sets on the business world.

In fact the indices you hear quoted are at best a partial way to measure the market. The Footsie usually refers to the **FTSE-100 index**, which is produced by the *Financial Times* and the London Stock Exchange – hence FT-SE. This measures the movement in the value of shares in the biggest 100 companies on the Exchange. It rises and falls each moment the stock market is open, as the prices of shares change. It started at 1,000 in January 1984 and today is around 6,000, showing that the value of these shares has gone up about six-fold in those 24 years. The FTSE-100 is an odd index. It uses the shares of the biggest 100 companies and every three months some companies that have fallen in value are booted out and others that have grown are added to it. It is also weighted so that a change in the value of shares in the biggest companies has a bigger effect on the index than changes in smaller companies.

Another index is the **FTSE All Share index.** Contrary to its name, it is not an index of the price of all the shares listed on the London Stock Exchange, but only of those in about 700 companies whose shares are actively traded. That is perhaps a better guide to the state of business in the UK, not least because many of the companies in the FTSE-100 are not really UK companies at all. They could be based in Russia or Hong Kong but want to have the kudos of being listed on the London Stock Exchange.

In New York the **Dow Jones Industrial Average** ('the Dow') is an index of just 30 typical large companies on the New York Stock Exchange and excludes those in transport or utilities. Another stock market in the USA, the **Nasdaq Composite Index** or Nasdaq, is an electronic stock exchange that measures the movement in the share prices of more than 5,000 companies that trade on it. In Japan, the **Nikkei Stock Average** takes 225 representative and actively traded shares on the Tokyo Stock Exchange.

These indices are seen as important because they indicate the value of shares as a whole (even though some of them in fact don't) and that is seen as reflecting what is often called the 'sentiment' of the market – which is a strange feeling to have for people whose only job is to buy cheap and sell dear and make absolutely nothing except money. The indices are also seen as reflecting the strength of the economy in the country where they are based. That can lead to rises or falls in the value of individual shares just because the UK, for example, is seen as a good – or a bad – place to do business. That is true even though a large proportion of the companies in the FTSE-100 are in fact owned abroad and trade mainly outside the UK. So it does not measure the health of the UK economy. It also excludes the growing number of companies that are privately owned. But rises or falls in the FTSE are seen as reflecting the health of the economy, which is why you will hear statements such as 'In the City the FTSE is up 43 points at 65 19'.

In truth, it is all fairly meaningless. First, newsreaders often do not make it clear it is the FTSE-100 they are quoting as opposed to the dozen or so other FTSE indices that exist. Second, they should not say 'sixty-five nineteen' but 'six thousand five hundred and nineteen'. Moreover, the number of points in the change is irrelevant. It is the percentage change that shows what is going on. A rise or fall of less than 1 per cent is negligible. Only a greater change and one that lasts for some days is really significant.

WHY SHARES ARE WIDELY RECOMMENDED

Given all the uncertainty attaching to shares, why does just about every financial adviser recommend that any money we have to invest should be put into shares?

There is one respectable reason. For most of the professional lives of the people involved investments in shares have been a one-way bet to make money. Research into investment performance going back more than a century, to 1899, shows that money invested in shares does grow more than money saved in bank accounts or invested in safe havens such as Government bonds.

This is particularly true over the last quarter of the last century. From 1975 to 1999 the price of shares in UK companies rose in every single year except three – and after each of those three years when prices fell they rose strongly the following year. Over that time share prices rose on average by 12.8 per cent a year. That was an amazing return on the money invested – clearly, a one-way bet. A whole generation of financial advisers had seen share prices do nothing but go up, year after year after year. The occasional stumble was nothing more than a temporary glitch. So it is not surprising that the advisers told everyone to put their money on the stock market.

But then came 2000. Prices fell. In 2001 they fell again, by more. Then in 2002 they fell again, by more still. Between their peak on 31 December 1999 and their low point in March 2003 share prices fell by more than half. But everyone took a deep breath and, lo and behold, they rose in 2004, 2005, 2006 and 2007. After four years of growth the falls of the early 21st century are beginning to look like another blip. So investing in shares is seen as a good way to make a bit more than putting your money in a savings account.

But there is another reason – one which most advisers prefer not to talk about. Putting their client's cash into shares is easy money for them. They earn good commission, and they are not likely to get into trouble for recommending a stock market investment because the consensus view is that it is a Good Thing.

FUNDS

An old boy scout trick is used to find the height of a building. You ask everyone in the group what they think it is and then average the results (one variation on this technique says you should exclude the biggest and the smallest guesses to leave out the jokers who say an inch or a mile). The average is always more accurate than just asking one person.

It is the same with shares. Although shares in Marks & Spencer or any other single company can rise and fall dramatically, if you look at shares as a whole they tend to rise and fall less erratically. So almost all stock market investment by individuals is into what are called funds. These funds consist of shares in lots of different companies and sometimes in different parts of the world. The hope is that when one company does badly another does well and it smooths out the ups and downs. So it protects you from some of the risk in investing in shares.

When you invest in a fund you buy a small chunk of that investment. Often these are called 'units', so you buy, say, 1,000 units at £1 each.

You can think of your investment as being money in a little pot with your name on it and there are 1,000 units in it. There is a lid on the top and you have the key to it. So only you can decide when you buy extra units to put in or when you sell those units and take some money out. But someone else is deciding what is in the units – in other words, where your money is actually invested.

There is also a little hole in the bottom with a small tap on it. Out of this hole your money slowly drips into the fund manager's hands. That drip happens on two occasions:

- once a year, when a percentage of the value of your fund will be siphoned off. This is called an annual management charge and it can be anything from 0.5 per cent to 4 per cent. So however much your fund might grow, as the shares grow this force drags it back as the fund manager takes a cut – a cut that will be taken whether your fund goes up or down. In other words, if they have done their job of managing your money so badly that it is worth less at the end of the year they will still take their cut as a percentage of what remains. So although you are protected from some of the risk of investing in shares, the funds are protected from all of it – they make money whether markets rise or fall. They just make a bit less when they fall because your money is worth a lot less and their percentage of that is worth a little less.
- as if the annual drain were not bad enough, you also lose

money every time you sell a unit to take money out, because in most funds units have two prices – a buying price and a selling price. You might buy 1,000 units for £1,000 but if you sell them immediately you will not get your £1,000 back. You will lose about 3 per cent – it varies from fund to fund and investment to investment. So you have to leave your money in for quite a while just to pay the difference between the buying and the selling price – 'the spread', as it is called in investment circles.

TYPES OF INVESTMENT FUND

There are two fundamental types of fund. Some are **managed** by experts supported by a large research department to study the whole market in shares. They visit major companies to assess how they are being run and take account of economic and other factors to decide where the best place is to invest. They then buy shares in those com-panies and hope their judgement is right (though of course they get paid whether they are right or not, so it is you who should really be hoping that they get it right).

Another type of fund simply relies on the fact that overall the average price of all shares tends to rise over time. So instead of employ-ing a large research department and doing all that expensive work and study, it simply spreads your money across the shares in every company. In that way they will follow the index of the whole market up – and, of course, down. They are called **trackers** because they fol-low or 'track' the market index.

Everyone agrees that trackers have one major advantage. They are cheaper to run. That is because they do not need expensive research departments and skilled managers. They just need to do a technical job. They see what shares are in a particular index and buy them in the right proportion. That cheapness is passed on to you in lower charges.

Also, there is a further advantage that people in the investment industry tend to be less forthcoming about. In the long term track-ers do better than managed funds. Of course, in any one year some managed funds will do better than a fund which tracks the market. In the jargon, they 'out-perform' the market. So if the FTSE-100, for example, rises by 12 per cent, funds that out-perform it will rise by more than 12 per cent. They might even manage to out-perform the market over five years or more. So good investing simply involves picking managed funds that consistently out-perform the market. Easy-peasy … just the same way that you make money on horses by backing a winner.

And that is the problem. Tomorrow you can always see what did well today. But yesterday it was more difficult. Research shows it is impossible to predict who will manage it next year, which is of course what you want to know. A good fund one year will not necessarily be a good fund the next year. There is no 'persistency', as it is called. Even a bright star rises and falls. However, research shows that one thing does pass on. Bad funds tend to stay bad funds. A dog is always a dog.

That is why the Financial Services Authority refuses to publish past performance statistics in its comparative tables of funds. A few years ago it also imposed very strict rules on how past performance was used in adverts. That is why you almost never see such performance figures quoted – because when they are presented honestly in a standard format few funds come out well.

Trackers of course by definition do as well as the market as a whole. They follow it up and they follow it down. But then so do most funds that are managed. In fact, every year trackers do better than most managed funds, and in the long term they do better than almost all of them.

Some people will tell you that although particular funds cannot be relied on, the people who manage them can. So if you moved your money from one fund to another as the manager moves – and gets paid loads more – you could hitch your investment wagon to a star. But not any more. Research published in July 2004 showed that out of 175 fund managers with a five-year track record, only 11, that is 6 per cent, managed to do better than the market average every year for five years. There is no evidence that even this élite will continue to do better in the future. So picking the manager who will do well over the next five years – which is what matters – is an impossible task.

All that means that if you want to hitch your investment fortunes to the wagon of the stock market the best way to do it is to go for a fund that tracks the market, and does so effectively but as cheaply as possible.

One way to do that – and in many ways the best – to buy into what is called an 'Exchange Traded Fund'. Although these are shares (one branded by Barclays is called iShares) they are essentially tracker funds with two big advantages:

1 the annual charge is very low

2 they have one price – there is no spread between buying and selling.

You can buy ETFs in almost any market in the world and you can go beyond shares and buy ETFs that track the price of gold or oil. If you want to stick to share trackers you can pick the FTSE-100 or the FTSE All Share in the UK, or you can splash a bit of money into the market anywhere from Japan to Switzerland. Alternatively, you can invest in what is called a 'sector' such as oil and gas, telecoms or small companies.

The main risk with ETFs is that you will pick wrong. Just because oil and gas or the Japanese stock market has done well in the last year or so does not mean it will do well next year. Just like managed funds, indices can go down as well as up and going up for a few years is no guarantee of going up the next.

Most amateur investors make that classic mistake. They watch prices in a particular investment rise and buy when they are high. Then they watch prices of some investments fall and panic and sell when they are low. But remember, investments are for the long term. If you go into the stock market you must have faith that overall in the long term the price of the shares will rise. If you just want to hitch your fortunes to the wagon of the FTSE All Share Index, ETFs are a cheap way to do it.

Apart from the fact that in the long run managed funds do no better than the stock market, the range of funds is so vast it is very difficult to make a rational choice. Of course, there are many different kinds of funds and they always seem to have funny names. You might be offered Leveraged High Yield, Perpetual Japanese, Emerging Markets. Some say they are invested in 'financial opportunities' or in 'new start-ups'. And some are clear about the kind of person they want to attract by using words like 'aggressive', 'special situations', 'dynamic' or 'cautious'. But the truth is that even when these words seem like ordinary English words that you can understand, in fact they are no more than marketing tools designed to make sure that there is something for everyone.

Worst of all are funds called 'higher yield' or 'higher income' or 'growth'. They represent the hopes or – as the promoters of them normally put it because they prefer long words to short ones – the aspirations of the investment company. They are not a promise and certainly not a guarantee. Don't try complaining that a growth fund has not grown or an income fund has produced no income. There are no guarantees – except of course that the amount you make is unpredictable and might be negative.

The one certainty is that the managers will take their percentage out of your fund every single year and regardless of how your investment has performed. Up or down, good or bad, excellent or disastrous, the annual charges will drip out of the bottom of your investment pot. And they are much bigger from a managed fund than the charges for a tracker or an ETF.

To be fair, running a managed fund is a very expensive business. There is a huge research department, a team of highly paid executives and of course the very highly paid manager. There are the costs of buying and selling investments as this top team decides to move your money around, and there is the money they lose on the spread – the difference between the buying price and the selling price. The question is whether that is money well spent.

So whereas a tracker fund should charge less than 1 per cent of your money every year – and an ETF will charge half that or less – a managed fund may charge 2 per cent a year or more. In addition they will often make a charge when you join the fund – perhaps 5 per cent of your money. So you give the fund £1,000 and it will actually invest just £950. Given that overall managed funds do not do any better than trackers, it is a waste of money.

So back to the question. Why do advisers keep recommending that we put money not only in shares but normally in managed funds rather than trackers or ETFs? One reason of course is that most of them have never known anything else. Another is that over the long term it has been good advice (the meaning of 'long term' will be discussed later). It is very hard to criticise an adviser who recommends a standard stock market investment. The adviser is just going with the consensus view.

Finally, there is the reason they never tell you. They get paid more commission for recommending stock market-based investments, and very often the riskier the investment the more they get paid. Putting your money in cash or National Savings & Investments earns them no commission. Nor do cheap investments such as ETFs. So human nature being what it is, advisers tend to prefer investments that pay them money.

COMMISSION

In ten years' time some future edition of this book may well be saying: 'Commission used to be a real problem in financial services but since it was banned in April 2015 by the Financial Services Authority life has got a lot simpler – and more honest.'

Of course, we cannot say that today. Commission is alive and well. But there is a growing feeling that commission will be banned – perhaps long before 2015.

This is why. Commission creates a conflict of interest between the financial adviser and you. Your interest is in buying the best-value product. But the adviser's interest is in selling you the product that makes the most commission. So whatever they sell you and however honest they are, you will always have a sneaking feeling – human nature being what it is – that you have been sold the product that is right for the adviser rather than you.

This is not normally a matter of dishonesty or cheating or deceit. It is simply because the pay structure of many financial sales staff – or 'advisers' – is such that if they don't sell they don't earn. Their basic pay is too low to live on so they have to sell the right stuff to earn enough to survive. Generally it is the system that is at fault, not the individuals.

The difficulty with getting rid of commission is that it is at the heart of the financial services industry – squeezing it hard. Of course, commission is at the heart of many retail businesses. Sales staff earn more the more they sell – but not everywhere. The computer retailer PC World scrapped commission across its 150 stores in March 2006 because the company realised that, as the company put it: 'The previous commission-based selling scheme encouraged behaviour that was not necessarily in the customer's interests.'

So the company piloted no commission – called One Team – and in stores where it was tried out performance as measured by converting visits to sales was up by 5 per cent compared with the stores where commission was still paid. Conclusion: paying no commission is better for staff, better for customers, and better for the company.

In financial services it is even more important not to sell customers the wrong thing than it is in high street retail, because financial products are not like a washing machine or a carpet:

- they are much more expensive
- they are much less easy to understand.
- it is much more difficult to see if anything goes wrong
- faults may not become apparent for many years
- when they do it may be too late to put things right
- it is much more difficult to get your money back.

Concerns about commission led the Financial Services Authority in 2005 to impose rules on advisers to make them tell us what they were earning from what they sold us. Unfortunately those rules were scrapped in November 2007 and replaced with much vaguer rules about what advisers have to tell us.

Commission rates vary from product to product and from time to time. If companies want to sell a particular product they will increase the commission paid on it. If they want to sell less of an unprofitable product commission is cut. Here are some examples of what commission might be.

If you invest a lump sum in a unit trust the adviser will get about 4 per cent of the money invested and then half a per cent a year of the value of the investment. So if you invest a lump sum of £10,000 the adviser will get £400 to start and then £50 a year for as long as you keep the investment going. If the investment grows, this annual commission will grow as well.

If you put money into a personal pension the adviser may get as much as 80 per cent of the first year's premiums in commission. In addition he or she will get an annual payment of perhaps half or even one per cent of the value of the fund. So every year a proportion of the money you pay in goes to pay the adviser's salary instead of building up your pension for the future. Even with stakeholder pensions, which should be cheaper, something like the first four months' contributions you pay do not go into the fund at all – instead, they go to your adviser, and you will be paying perhaps £3 of every £1,000 in your pension fund to your adviser every year until you retire.

These annual commissions – also called renewal or trail commission – are supposed to encourage your sales rep to keep in touch and review your finances – to act, in other words, like a real financial adviser – the title most of them adopt but few really fulfil. Too many of them simply take the money and run. The only time you are likely to hear from them is when they want to sell you something else.

AVOIDING COMMISSION

Commission – and the bias it causes – is hard to avoid. But there are two ways to do it.

All independent financial advisers have to offer you the choice of paying them a fee rather than commission. If you go for a fee of course you avoid commission bias – the commission is either not paid at all or, if it is, it is paid to you rather than the adviser. But the problem is that fees are expensive. That is not to say that some advisers are not worth £100 an hour or even the £200 an hour some will charge you. But if they take five hours on your case could you afford to pay £500 or £1,000 for their time? Most people could not – or would not want to.

There is a way out of this conundrum, which was piloted by Scottish Life and is now promoted in one way or another by several consumer organisations. You agree on the appropriate product. The adviser says that will cost you £X for his fee. You are then loaned the money to pay the fee over one, two or even five years. That separates the price of the product from the price of the advice and gives you a way to pay for it – just as you might buy a sofa or a car with a bank loan or an expensive new suit on your credit card.

This simple idea has been hijacked by the financial services industry and it is now called 'customer-agreed remuneration' (CAR) which, typically for financial services, is a grand and inaccurate name for a simple idea.

It works like this. The financial product is priced without any fee or commission for the adviser. The adviser then says, 'My advice will cost you £450.' You agree to that, and you pay for it in one of three ways: you write a cheque; you borrow the money – perhaps by paying with a credit card; or the fee is added to the cost of the product. And that is the dangerous bit. The fee might be paid by instalments over years and years of the life of the financial product, which means you are borrowing the cost over many years and that makes it very expensive.

So if you are offered CAR always pay for it by cheque or a short-term loan, not over the 40-year life of a pension. Otherwise, CAR is just the new way of paying commission by calling it a fee. It does not avoid commission. So reject it.

There is another way to get products without commission, but it means making all your own choices without any advice. Because of the weird way financial services works you still have to go through someone called a financial adviser, even if they give you no advice. They are called 'discount brokers' or 'money supermarkets'. Commission is still paid: like the tide, you cannot stop it – you just have to manage things to accommodate it. Then the adviser gives almost all of it back to you. They can afford to do that because they do not give you advice – they just do what you ask. You decide what you need and what to buy and they take no responsibility for it. You can invest in anything including shares or unit trusts. These discount brokers operate through the internet and their websites will give you general guidance – not advice, of course – about investment and risk. This information may not always be very balanced or comprehensive.

Similar to discount brokers are fund supermarkets, but they tend to charge more and let you have a more limited range of products.

FINDING A FINANCIAL ADVISER

How do you find a good plumber? *Yellow Pages*? Personal recommendation from a friend? Ask another tradesman? Finding a good financial adviser is just as difficult but you can improve your chances.

First, the rules.

There are at the moment broadly three kinds of financial adviser. A financial adviser can be:

- tied to one bank or insurance company and only allowed to sell their products
- tied to a small number of banks and insurance companies and only allowed to sell their products
- independent of banks and insurance companies and not only able but required by law to find the best product for the customer from the whole market.

Obviously you should only ever consider independents. No other adviser can give you the best advice because he or she is confined to a limited list of products. It would be like going to a Toyota dealership and being surprised that you came out with a Toyota. So reject all blandishments from banks, building societies or insurance companies to take 'advice' from one of their 'financial advisers'. They are sales staff for that company's products – nothing more, nothing less.

However, that still leaves about 20,000 independents to choose from. Step forward the internet, and specifically the oddly titled website www.unbiased.co.uk. In truth, it is a way of finding local independent financial advisers by certain criteria. Everyone on it is independent, and you can specify what qualifications the adviser should have. You can also say whether you would prefer a male or female adviser and how you want to pay. You will then be shown a small number of the IFAs who fulfil your criteria and are near to where you live. Of course, being on the list does not mean they are all good IFAs. But by specifying the qualifications it gives you a fighting chance.

Go and visit two or three of them – the first visit will be free – and see if you like them.

This book can give only general advice on choosing an IFA. But here is one thing to beware of. If you ask your financial adviser about stock market investments they will always ask about your attitude to risk. Sometimes in that grandiose way the financial services industry has they will ask about your appetite for risk or ask what your 'risk profile' is. Often they will preface that by talking of the 'risk reward trade-off' and perhaps add 'You've got to take a risk to get the reward'. The way many advisers talk of it, you would think it was a one-way bet. You take something called a 'risk' and you will get a reward. But of course risk does not mean that. Risk means you can lose money as well as make it. Otherwise there is no risk. Strangely, that downside is never mentioned much.

Here is a way to assess your 'risk profile'. You have £1,000. You give it to a financial company and in a year's time you have only £600. How will you feel?

Terrible – I worked hard for that money and I did not want it lost to someone else, whether through commission or poor investment.

A bit upset – I was told it was a risk but I did not really expect to lose money. You don't, do you?

Quite happy – I knew I could lose it but I also knew there was a chance I could make more than I could in a savings account. It was a bet. I lost. Some you win, some you lose.

If you answered 'c' then you are a true stock market investor. If you ticked 'a' you should put your money in the best savings account you can find and not go near a financial adviser. If you put 'b' you still haven't understood what risk means. Risk means you could lose your money. And it might happen – even over the long term.

THE LONG TERM

This section began with a warning that 'investment is for the long term' – and it is. But what is the long term? Advisers often suggest the long term is as short as five years. But that is not right.

If you picked a period of five years at random in the last hundred and you invested evenly across all the companies listed on the London stock market you would have one chance in three of ending up no better off at the end. Of course, you would have two chances in three of making money – sometimes not very much, sometimes a lot. But a one-in-three chance of losing money is not very good. Of course, these figures relate to the whole of the 20th century and a bit more, and most of the bad times were a long time ago in the first half of that period.

But even in the recent past you can see the danger. Between 1999 and 2006 – a period of seven years – the money you invested would be worth just about the same at the end as it was at the beginning. Even by the end of 2007 – when the market had risen for four years in a row – the average return on your money would have been just over 1.5 per cent a year. You would have done better to find the best cash account and keep it in there.

So how long is long-term? After ten or even 15 years the odds shorten to about one chance in four of ending up no better off and after 15 years the chances are much the same: just three chances in four of making money. Again, taking the last ten years, which takes us through the highs of 1999 and the lows of 2003, the average annual return on your money was just 3.4 per cent.

On the other hand, a hundred years definitely is long-term. Over the last hundred years stock market-based investments have done better than investments in other things. Unfortunately, we do not have that long. However, 25 years is not much worse. Over 25 years making money in the stock market has been pretty much a dead cert since 1900. But much less than 25 and there is a real risk you will end up worse-off – or at least no better off – than when you started. That view was supported by the Financial Services Authority in 2003 when the general manager of its investment business said, 'Basically, long term . . . is 20 to 25 years'.

So when a financial adviser tells you that long term means 'at least five years and perhaps ten' remind them of what the regulator said in 2003. If they then say that that was a particularly difficult period for stock market investments and everyone was a bit pessimistic, ask if he or she knows how many times an investment spread across the stock market has gone down, rather than up, over a five-year period in the last hundred years. You now know it is one out of three. The adviser will not. Then hit them with this quote from the Financial Services Authority in a 2004 report: 'Over an even shorter time frame [than five years] the equity market is more like a game of chance than an investment.' (This was in the *Projections Review – the case for change*, July 2004, Annex 4, page 2.) Oh, and 'equity' means 'shares'.

INFLATION

There is one final card an adviser might play to encourage investment: inflation. You put your money in cash, take out the interest earned as income, and in 30 years' time your savings will be worth half as much because inflation has eaten away at them. So why take that risk?

The truth is more complicated, however. Yes, inflation is the enemy of saving. But it is also the enemy of investing. Money invested declines in value just as much as money in savings. Of course, with investment the hope is that it will grow more than money that is just saved. But as we have seen that is not guaranteed and is certainly not always the case. So inflation is irrelevant to the decision about whether to save or invest: it is a constant drain on your money whatever you do with it.

CONCLUSION

This book is not advising you against investing. But if you do invest you must embark on it with your eyes open. Investment is for the long term. Investment is risky (and that means you can lose as well as gain). It is for money you do not need for a long time and at a pinch could lose. ∎

6

PENSIONS

Pensions get their own chapter even though they are just another investment – in some ways the ultimate investment. They are exactly what investment should be: long-term, and subsidised. Yes, subsidised. Because for every £100 you save the Chancellor pops in another £25 – unless you are lucky enough to pay higher-rate tax (well, an income of more than £41,000 a year is quite lucky, isn't it?), when he makes you even better off by chucking in £67 for every £100 you pay in.

So pensions almost always mean investing in shares. First, putting money into a pension is almost always a long-term investment (though not quite so long-term by the time you are in your 50s). Secondly, the subsidy means that even if the value of your investments goes down (and it can) you have a margin of money from other taxpayers before you start losing money you have spent yourself.

Huge tomes have been written on pensions, yet still they have not covered everything. The legislation itself runs to thousands of pages. This chapter will concentrate on the most important aspects, not the detail.

It is one of the strange natural laws of the universe that where there are pensions there is jargon. Sometimes pensions seem to generate more words than they do money – hence the weird and sometimes confusing words scattered through this chapter, which will be explained along the way.

PENSIONS AT WORK

If you have paid into a pension at work you are lucky. This type of pension (known as occupational, company or employer's) is the best sort. They come in two main types – very good and OK.

SALARY-RELATED PENSION SCHEMES
The best schemes pay you a pension at retirement which is related to how much you earned at work. Usually they pay a proportion of your final year's pay for each year you have paid into the scheme. Most

of them pay you either 1/60th of your pay for each year or 1/80th. But they can pay anything from a very generous 1/30th to a rather mean 1/120th. So if you have paid in for 40 years you will get two-thirds or a half (40/60ths or 40/80ths) of your pay when you retire. The way your final years' salary is worked out varies from scheme to scheme. It can literally be your pay in the final year before you retire. Or it can be an average or the highest of the last three years or so.

Recently some companies have changed the calculation so you get a proportion of your average salary over the whole time you have paid into the scheme. Each year's pay is revalued for inflation before it is averaged. Overall, average pay schemes pay lower pensions and that saves money. But for people whose pay peaks in their 40s rather than towards the end of their career it can mean a bigger pension than a final salary scheme. Nowadays schemes that pay a pension related to salary are called 'defined benefit' or DB schemes. That phrase is used because with these schemes it is the amount of the pension that is paid which is guaranteed (not to mention that it is almost unintelligible outside the pensions world).

Paying a pension related to salary is a very expensive promise for the future. The cost is hard to estimate because it depends on three unknowns:

1 how the contributions paid into the scheme will grow over the years until you retire

2 how much your pay will be at the end of your career

3 how long you will live (see pages 226–8 for more on longevity).

As a result the average amount paid into salary-related pensions is high – 20.4 per cent of pay in 2007. Most of this, 16 per cent, is paid by the employer and just 4.4 per cent is paid by employees. So it is a real bargain. You get a guaranteed pension and four-fifths of the cost is paid by your employer.

Because salary-related pensions are expensive they are getting rarer among private companies. But in the public sector – the civil service, teaching, higher education, the National Health Service, the police and fire service, local government and so on – they are still almost universal.

If your employer offers a salary-related scheme, join it. In exchange for a modest contribution you will be given a salary-related, index-linked pension for life. You can't go wrong, even if you are already in your 50s.

Some salary-related pension schemes will let you buy what are called 'added years'. If you joined the scheme when you were, say, 30 years old, you can buy extra years so that your benefits are counted as if you had had an extra year in the scheme. In other words, instead of getting, say, a pension of 30/80ths of your pay you will get 31/80ths or, if you pay for five 'added years', 35/80ths. It is usually a very good deal, especially in your 50s as there is less time to wait to get the pension. Many employers will let you pay for the added years over a period by deduction from your pay. Like all pension contributions they are tax-free.

PENSION POT SCHEME

The other sort of scheme does not promise you any particular pension when you retire. Instead, the money you and your employer pay into the scheme is invested in a pension fund and you own a small share of that fund. Hence the phrase 'pension pot'. It is not a great name but it is better than the official terms, which are 'money purchase' or 'defined contribution' – inevitably abbreviated to DC – which are pretty meaningless.

It is best to think of it as a pot in which the contributions paid by you and your employer are saved up. Far less goes into these schemes than into salary-related schemes. The average is a total of 9 per cent, with 6.3 per cent paid by the employer and 2.7 per cent by employees.

As these schemes are so much cheaper than salary-related schemes many employers have closed their salary-related schemes – either for all staff or just for new staff – and replaced them with a pension pot scheme.

If your employer offers a pension pot scheme that it pays into the general rule is to join it. The percentage the employer is paying into your pension is free money. What you pay in is of course further subsidised by a contribution from the Treasury.

PERSONAL ACCOUNTS

At the moment not every employer offers a pension scheme that they pay into. About 6 million people work for such employers, which are often small companies. That is scheduled to change from April 2012. From that date – which, we have been warned, may slip by a year – almost everyone in work will automatically be enrolled into either an existing company scheme or into a new national pension scheme which at the moment is called 'personal accounts', though that rather silly name may change too.

Anyone who is automatically enrolled will have the right to opt back out. However, if they do they will again be put back in every time they change jobs or, if they stay with the same employer, every three years.

People under the age of 22 or over pension age and those earning less than £90 a week will not be automatically enrolled but can join, and if they do an employer's contribution must be paid. Self-employed people will also be able to join if they choose, though of course there will be no contribution from an employer. The government hopes that inertia will mean that most people stay in the scheme and that millions who do not pay into a pension at work will in future do so.

The new personal accounts will be a pension pot scheme, but the contribution level will be lower than the average that goes into existing pension pot schemes. The government says the total contribution put into personal accounts will eventually be 8 per cent of pay. But the employer will put in the smaller share – just 3 per cent – while the employee will put in 5 per cent, of which 1 per cent will be the state tax subsidy. In fact, these quoted percentages are not of the whole salary, just of a band of pay which will probably run from about £6,000 to about £40,000 a year. So the percentage of total pay going into the scheme will be less than 7 per cent and for someone on average pay not much more than 6 per cent. Moreover, when the scheme begins these contributions will be lower – 1 per cent each in the first year rising to the full amount in year 3.

So not very much money will go into the new scheme. That leads to the big problem with it. Some people will pay into this scheme –

which is, after all, compulsory unless you choose to opt out – but end up no better off. That is because the modest pension they will get out of it may be no higher than they could get if they did not pay into the scheme and then claimed all the means-tested benefits they were entitled to. The people particularly at risk of being no better off include those in their 50s when the new scheme begins, as they will not have long to build up a pension. It also applies to people whose income will be low enough in retirement for them to claim Pension Credit and Council Tax Benefit. That applies even more to people who live in rented accommodation and who can get help with their rent through Housing Benefit. The government has yet to announce how, or indeed whether, it will identify people who will be no better off if they stay in the scheme or whether it will warn them to leave.

PERSONAL PENSIONS

No financial product has been as widely mis-sold as personal pensions. Commission was largely to blame, together with shameless government promotion of what was, in 1988, a brand new idea – pensions for all. Nearly 2 million people were mis-sold personal pensions between 1988 and 1994, as a result of which the financial services industry was forced to pay out £11.5 billion in compensation and spend £2 billion more to run the compensation scheme. In general, personal pensions – and 'stakeholder' pensions, which are just a type of personal pension – are fine if you do not have a pension at work which your employer pays into. They are also fine to top up a pension at work if you need to do that. What you should never do – and what was behind most of the mis-selling – is to use a personal pension to replace an employer's pension.

'Stakeholder' pensions are the only sort of personal pension you should consider. They have low charges – the lower the better – and rules which make them flexible and as safe as any investment based on shares can be. By law their charge must be limited to 1.5 per cent of your fund each year. You can find lower charges than that. The FSA comparison site is a good place to find the lowest charges. You can also stop and start contributions and move your fund to another provider without penalty. Many financial advisers will not be that keen to sell stakeholder pensions as they earn very little from them.

Since October 2001 every employer has had to offer access to a stakeholder scheme for their employees. But they have not had to pay into the scheme and take-up has been tiny. They are now moribund pending the introduction of personal accounts.

SHOULD I PAY INTO A PENSION?

Even in your 50s it is not too late to pay into a pension, though normally you should expect to leave the money in for at least ten years. You can now pay in as much as you earn in the year if you want to. Even if you have no earnings you can pay in up to £3,600. In fact you write a cheque for £2,880 and the other £720 comes as a gift from the Chancellor. The money will be invested by your personal pension provider and after investment growth and minus the annual charge you should have a reasonable little pension pot after ten years.

There is also a useful trick you can adopt once you are 50 to boost the amount in your pension at no cost to yourself.

You start a new personal pension and write a cheque to My New Pension Fund for £800. The Chancellor immediately gets out his cheque book and writes a cheque to Your New Pension Fund for £200. So there is £1,000 in there. But as you are already 50 you can immediately declare what is poetically called a 'benefit crystallisation event'. That is the new term for 'retirement' but nowadays it does not mean you have to stop work or stop paying into your fund. You decide at any age from 50 (that rises to 55 from 6 April 2010) when your benefit crystallisation event is and you can take out a quarter of your fund in cash. So your fund writes you a cheque for £250. That leaves a pension fund of £750 which has cost you just £800 − £250 = £550. So for every £100 you have put in there is in fact £136 in your fund. If you want you can then put that tax-free cash straight back into your pension.

And yes, the Chancellor will give you a bit more. You can do this several times. It is called recycling and there are limits on it – never take out a cash lump sum for more than £16,500 is the easiest one to remember.

But in fact you do not need to recycle at all. All you need to do is decide how much you can afford to put in your pension. Say that is £1,000. Add 45.5 per cent and write out a cheque to your pension fund for £1,455. The Chancellor adds £364 so your fund is £1,819 and you claim back your 25 per cent tax-free which is £455. That leaves your fund at £1,364 and the cost to you has been £1,000 (all figures rounded to nearest pound).

If you are a higher-rate taxpayer the arithmetic is even better. You can safely write a cheque for almost 2.3 times the amount you really want to pay into your pension. Again, suppose you think you can afford about £1,000. You write a cheque for £2,286, the Chancellor writes one for £571. You take back tax-free cash of £714 and then reclaim higher-rate tax of £572. So you have spent £2,286 − £714 − £572 = £1,000 and in your fund is £2,143. It isn't magic, just benefit crystallisation!

Of course, once money is in a pension fund you are limited in what you can do with it. The money left in the fund can just stay there and grow – you can even pay more in if you want. If the fund grows you can take 25 per cent of the growth as another tax-free lump sum at a later date. You can decide when to convert it into a pension or draw an income from it right up to the age of 75.

TRIVIAL PENSIONS

If you haven't saved very much in a pension scheme you may have what is called a 'trivial' pension fund. That means your total pension fund is £16,500 or less (in 2008/9 or £17,500 in 2009/10). If your fund is called 'trivial' then you do not have to convert it into a pension. You can take the whole lot out in cash and do what you want with it. A quarter of the fund can be taken tax-free. The rest is taxable – don't complain, you paid no tax on the way in so the Revenue taxes you on the way out just as it would if you did convert it to a pension.

The way it is taxed is this. The balance of the fund is added to your income in the year you cash it in. It is then treated as earned income and taxed through PAYE before it is paid to you. So some or all of it may be taxed at 20 per cent or even 40 per cent if it takes you above the limit for higher-rate tax. If you have more than one fund you have to cash them all in within 12 months but you can arrange things so that they fall into two tax years to reduce the tax.

The limit for a trivial pension fund applies only if the total of all your work and personal pensions comes to £16,500 or less. If you have an entitlement to a salary-related pension, that is converted into a pension fund amount by multiplying the annual pension due by 20. So an annual pension of £500 counts as a pension fund of 20 x £500 = £10,000. Not all company pension schemes will let you cash in a trivial pension.

LARGER PENSION FUNDS

If your total pension funds come to more than the trivial limit then you will normally convert your fund into a pension. The normal way to do that is by buying an annuity. You give the money to an insurance company and it promises you an income for life. The thing many people hate about annuities that your pension fund belongs to the insurance company, not you. When you die, the company keeps whatever is left and there is nothing to pass on to your heirs. So it is a gamble. If you die shortly after taking out the annuity, the insurance company wins. If you live to be 120, you win. You can reduce the risk of a big loss by guaranteeing that the payments will be made to your heirs for at least five years, even if you die in that time. The extra cost is negligible – and recommended if you have heirs.

Buying an annuity is a once-and-for-all decision. You cannot go back on it. So it is vital to get it right. Choosing the wrong annuity can cost you a lot of money. The company that runs your pension will always try to keep you as a customer in retirement. But staying with them is usually a mistake. You should take advantage of what is called the open market option and use your fund to buy an annuity from the best provider available at the time. The one exception to that rule is if you pay into a pension that comes with a guaranteed annuity which may be paid at a rate well above the market level. If you do, stick with that. Before choosing the annuity provider there are two big decisions to make.

Single or joint If you have a spouse or partner who is financially dependent on you, you will probably want to ensure they will inherit part of your pension. That will of course reduce the pension paid to you. Also, if your partner dies first it will be money wasted. Like everything in pensions it is a gamble. A pension for your partner of two-thirds of yours will reduce the amount you get by about 10 per cent for a man aged 65.

Flat or rising Your annuity can be fixed for life, or it can rise each year either with inflation or by a fixed percentage such as 3 per cent. That will cut the amount you get at the start. An inflation-proofed pension will be about a third less at 65, one that rises by 3 per cent about a quarter less. You will have to live a very long time to get more money in total out of the pension that starts lower and rises. On the other hand, if you choose a flat pension you will be better off in the early years, but if you live a long time your income will decline in real terms, perhaps halving over 20 years.

BUYING AN ANNUITY

Before buying an annuity it is best to talk to a specialist independent financial adviser, particularly if you have any health issues. A good independent adviser will find the best annuity for your particular circumstances. You can see roughly what you would get by using the comparative tables published by the Financial Services Authority or the simpler but slightly less comprehensive commercial website at www.annuitydirect.co.uk.

You should also consider whether you can get your pension boosted by your health or lifestyle. Some providers give more to smokers, because they tend to die younger: this can boost your annuity by 15 per cent. One annuity provider also announced recently that it would consider life expectancy by postcode and pay more to people in areas where life expectancy was short.

Most of us understate bad health when we talk to an insurance company. But when you buy an annuity you should be completely honest about any health problems, worries or tests that you have had. The less healthy you appear, the more you will get. Serious health issues can double the annuity you are paid. Some companies will offer you a non-guaranteed annuity linked to the stock market or other investments: they are not a good idea.

However much you have in your pension fund, the chances are that you will find the annuity you are offered disappointing. The younger you are, the more disappointing it will be. A man aged 65 can reckon on getting only about £7,000 for each £100,000 in the fund – and most people have a lot less than £100,000. Women get less because they live longer, about £6,500 for each £100,000 they have saved up. At 60 you will get about 10 per cent less; at 70 about 15 per cent more. Needless to say, if you try to buy an annuity in your 50s it will be even less. At 50 reckon on about £5,700 for a man or £5,500 for a woman. All those figures are the best on the market – the worst can be 10 per cent lower or even less. So finding the best is vital to maximise your retirement income.

Although most people buy an annuity you do not have to until you are 75. Instead you can just draw income from your fund. It is called an unsecured pension and the maximum amount is fixed by a weird formula. You can take less than the maximum or nothing at all, leaving your pension fund to grow. At the start of 2008 the maximum was £8,280 a year for a man of 65 and £7,800 for a woman per £100,000 in the fund. Once you have taken an unsecured pension it remains fixed for five years. If you die the balance in your pension fund – less 35 per cent tax – can form part of your estate and be left to your heirs.

Once you reach 75 the rules change. You can still draw an income – though now it is called an 'alternatively secured pension' – but the amount is much less, so most people would prefer to convert their fund into an annuity. At the start of 2008 the maximum for a £100,000 fund was £8,910 for a man and £7,830 for a woman aged 75. On death, any remaining funds can be left to a dependant's pension or to charity, but if you leave them to anyone else they will be taxed at 70 per cent.

There is a danger that if you take the maximum unsecured pension up to 75 and then the maximum alternatively secured pension after that, the money in your pension fund will run out before you die.

The Pensions Advisory Service is the best place for general advice on pensions (see chapter 14).

PENSION TRACING

In the distant past, if you left your job your pension usually died with it. But for many years now people who leave a job have been able either to take their pension with them or leave it to grow and claim it at retirement. Nowadays you can do that after as little as six months in the job. So people who have had several jobs can find they have various pensions due when they retire. Of course, many of us lose track of these pensions over the years. Fortunately the Pension Tracing Service can help reunite you with a pension you may have almost forgotten about.

The more information you can give, the better the chance of tracking down your pension. You will need the name and, if possible, address of any employer who might have run a scheme you belonged to. Dates when you joined and left the scheme – or worked for the company – will also help. You can also use the service to track down a personal pension you paid into yourself. You will need the name of the insurance company it was with or the adviser who sold it to you.

If the Pension Tracing Service cannot track down the pension, you could try the Unclaimed Assets Register, www.uar.co.uk, which will charge you £35 for tracing an old pension.

Just because you paid into a pension does not mean there is any money waiting for you. You may have had your contributions refunded. Before April 1975 you normally got all your contributions back when you left and up to April 1988 you could get a refund of contributions if you left the job before you had been there five years. After that the period was reduced to two years. After 1988 it is also possible that the pension was transferred to a new employer. For more information see

www.thepensionservice.gov.uk/atoz/atozdetailed/pensiontracing.asp

7

YOUR HOME

YOUR HOME

People in their 50s own most of the wealth in the UK. Much of that is tied up in their homes. Thirty years ago room sizes were bigger, gardens were standard and prices were affordable. The nice old family home you live in could be worth a fortune – literally. But unlocking that money, or some of it, is difficult.

That task is not helped by the almost complete indifference from the financial services industry. In 2007 it at last invented a word for this time of life – decumulation. It is a new word that you will not find in many dictionaries. But it will soon be there. As you may have guessed it is the opposite of 'accumulation'. When you are at work you use the income you earn to build up possessions. You accumulate stuff. But when you ease off on work you have less income and may well turn to those capital goods to provide an income. You stop accumulating and start to 'decumulate'. In other words you convert some of your capital goods – of which your home is by far the biggest – into an income you can use.

It is a simple idea and now there is a word for it. But it is hard to do – at least, it is in your 50s. Once you are 80 or even 70 you can use well-tried ways to raise money on your home. They are usually called 'equity release' products and we will look at those in more detail later. But in your 50s you are too young for equity release.

There are two alternatives. The first is moving. You probably do not want to move, your friends are all nearby, it is handy for your family, you really love the area, and although the old place is a bit big it really comes into its own at Christmas. All this is code of course for 'I really love this house and feel at home here' – which is fair enough. But let's look at the economics of moving to somewhere smaller.

TRADING DOWN

The simple way to release money from your home is to sell it and buy a cheaper one. Even this is not without cost – estate agents, lawyers, surveyors and of course removal contractors all know that moving is a time when large amounts of money pass through our hands just when we are feeling anxious and stressed and strict deadlines have to be met. So they respond to this human vulnerability by charging as much as they can get away with. Not to be outdone, the Chancellor has jumped on the gravy train by raising the cost of stamp duty, which is charged whenever property changes hands. But despite all these costs, trading down is still the cheapest and best way to release value from your home. So what will it cost?

SELLING YOUR HOME

Most people in England, Wales and Northern Ireland use an estate agent. In Scotland the solicitor usually acts as the estate agent as well as doing the legal work.

Despite the attractions of property websites and private sales the truth is that an agent's contacts, advertising, and ability to get your property in all the online sites make using an agent almost inevitable. Your estate agent will charge you a percentage of the price of the home. Reckon on 2–3 per cent – more if you do not give one agent exclusive rights to market it. Try to bargain them down. They know as well as you do that rising house prices have pushed up their fees dramatically although they are doing exactly the same amount of work as before. Some agents are springing up that charge the unthinkable – a fixed fee rather than a percentage. But normally, with the average price of a home touching £200,000, you can reckon on £5,000 for fees. Make sure that the fee is inclusive – you do not want to find you have to pay for photographs, valuation or advertising on top.

You will also need a solicitor to make sure your transfer of the property happens legally. That will cost you at least £400 for the conveyancing itself. Often it will be more, especially if the new home is expensive. You do not have to use a solicitor who is local either to you or the new home. If you are buying in a city you can sometimes save money by using a solicitor in a country town. In Scotland the solicitor will normally be the estate agent and will be local.

HOME INFORMATION PACKS

Nowadays every home that is marketed in England or Wales needs a Home Information Pack, or HIP. It contains:

- the documents which show you have the legal title to the property (though in fact that is all done electronically now)
- an energy performance certificate that will rate your home's energy efficiency from A (good) to G (poor), and
- the local authority and other searches that show a road is not about to be built through it.

That is all useful for the buyer. But you have to pay for it – reckon on £400. Normally the HIP will be produced by your estate agent, who may offer it free or cut-price.

But beware. If the sale does not go ahead or you do not use that agent for the sale you may have to pay the full cost. In Scotland and Northern Ireland you do not need a HIP, but a similar **Home Report** will start in Scotland at the end of 2008.

BUYING A HOME

Despite the HIP your solicitor will probably want to do the searches again and you have to pay the Land Registry fee to record the change of ownership. You can reckon on £1,200 or so for the legal costs of buying a home. The cost will be higher in cities, especially London, and the South East of England, but again you can shop around and find a solicitor anywhere in the country to do your conveyancing.

If you are buying on a mortgage the lender will demand a survey. But that is just for a valuation to make sure that the loan is a good risk. Although you pay, this survey will tell you nothing that you want to know. For a real survey you have to pay extra. It can cost about £400 but it is worth it. Apart from anything else it may help you haggle down the price – and make rather than cost you money. You can also use the buyer's HIP to haggle with – if the energy rating is low, ask for a discount so you can install an efficient boiler or insulation.

The removal company will also want paying. The cost depends on how much stuff you have, what service you want, and how far you are moving. But reckon on £500 to £1,000. If you have to store your possessions to cover the gap between buying and selling that can cost up to £100 a week.

You will also have to pay Stamp Duty Land Tax (SDLT).

STAMP DUTY LAND TAX 2007/8

Price of property	Rate of tax
Up to £125,000	nil
£125,001– £250,000	1 per cent of total price
£250,001– £500,000	3 per cent of total price
£500,001 and above	4 per cent of total price

SDLT is a strange tax. Once you cross a threshold it is calculated at that rate on the whole price. So if you buy a home for £250,000 the SDLT is 1 per cent or £2,500. But if the house costs £250,001 the SDLT is 3 per cent of that, which is £7,505. In other words, £1 on the price puts an extra £5,005 on the tax. (The odd fiver comes about because SDLT is always rounded up to the next £5.)

There are two ways to keep down the cost of SDLT.

In some parts of the country the nil rate of SDLT applies up to £150,000 instead of £125,000. It is called 'Disadvantaged Areas Relief' and you can check whether the property you are buying is in one by entering its postcode on HM Revenue website www.hmrc.gov.uk/so/dar/dar-search.htm. If your property is in one of these areas – and many of them are very attractive, despite the name – and costs between £125,000 and £150,000, you can save up to £1,500.

The other way to cut the tax is to negotiate with the owner to buy things such as carpets, curtains and other movable fittings separately – no tax is due on what you pay for them. This tip can be particularly useful if the cost of the property you are buying is just above one of the thresholds and you can bring the price down below the threshold. That will save you £5,005. But even if you do not cross a threshold you can still save money. For example, if you pay £2,000 for the carpets, curtains and the large table left in the dining room that would save £60 SDLT for a house in the middle band. Generally you can pay separately for items that can be moved. Fixed items such as a fitted kitchen or carpet count as part of the house and cannot be separated from the purchase price. Do not be tempted to pay more than these items are worth. The Revenue may well investigate deals, especially around the thresholds. The buyer is responsible for assessing the amount of SDLT correctly and paying it.

COST OF MOVING HOME (costs may differ in Scotland)			
	Old home £300,000	New home £200,000	Profit 100,000
Solicitor	£400	£1,200	
Estate agent	£7,500		
HIP	£400		
Survey		£400	
SDLT		£2,000	
Moving		£600	
Total	£8,300	£4,200	£12,500
Net profit			**£87,500**

So selling a home for £300,000 and buying one for £200,000 could easily cost you £12,500, leaving you with a net profit of £87,500 to use for your future. Although spending £12,500 may seem a lot, in fact it is still the cheapest way to release value from your home. Also, you can cut all these costs if you are prepared to do more work yourself – from advertising it in the paper to hiring a van for the move. You can even do the conveyancing if you want.

Just what £87,500 will buy you for your retirement will be examined later.

RENTING OUT A ROOM

The other way to make money from your home is to take in a lodger. Rent from a lodger is completely free of tax as long as it does not exceed £4,250 in the tax year. That is equivalent to rent of around £81.50 a week or £354 a month. To qualify, the person has to be a lodger rather than a tenant. That means they share some rooms with you – kitchen or bathroom or living rooms – and maybe eat with you from time to time.

This concession is called the Rent a Room scheme and you do not even have to tell the Revenue about the rent as long as it comes within this limit. You can use the scheme even if the lodger is a member of the family, as long as it is a genuine financial arrangement.

If the rent goes over £4,250 tax will be due. You can pay tax on the excess over £4,250 or work out your profit from the whole deal and pay tax on that. When you calculate your profit you can offset against the rent all the costs of letting the room. That will include a share of the costs of gas and electricity, water charges, insurance, Council Tax and any costs associated with finding or managing the lodgers. You can also set aside an amount for maintenance and repairs. If you have a mortgage you can charge a share of that too. But you must tell your insurance company and your lender that you are letting out a room. Your insurance will not normally cover the lodger's possessions.

Although all this sounds like tax-free money there are costs and disadvantages. Even if you stick within the tax-free £4,250 limit, you may have to pay Capital Gains Tax (CGT) if you sell your home and it has increased in value while you had the lodger. In practice if you have just let one room under the Rent a Room scheme it is unlikely that you will have to pay CGT. But if you were letting out several rooms CGT may have to be paid. No CGT charge can arise on the part of the property you let to a family member.

You must make sure that the lodger does not become a tenant. That means you must retain the right to enter their room – to clean or to make the bed, for example. Once the lodger has exclusive rights to their room they may be on the road to becoming a tenant. That can make it far harder to make them leave when you want. As a lodger under licence they have the right to stay only as long as the rent is paid. If the rent is paid monthly in advance they will only have the right to stay until the end of the month. Tenants have greater and more formal rights and although you can get rid of them it may require court action.

You must also make sure that any gas appliances the lodger uses conform to safety rules. You need to have an annual safety check by a registered contractor. Electrical items that you supply must also be safe to use, as must any electrical supply used by the lodger.

If you lived alone before letting the room, the 25 per cent discount on your Council Tax will normally stop from the time the lodger moves in. However, if the lodger is in a category which is exempt from Council Tax – such as a student – the discount will continue (see page 40). Any income you get from a lodger will normally reduce your entitlement to means-tested benefits or tax credits.

Find out more at www.direct.gov.uk and search for 'letting rooms in your home'.

EQUITY RELEASE

If you do not want to move or take in lodgers you may be tempted by 'equity release'. It is called that because it releases or frees up some of the value or 'equity' in your home. These products are only suitable for people of 70 or more, although some companies will sell them to people in their mid-50s.

There are two main sorts of equity release product.

A **lifetime mortgage** is the most common type. You borrow money against the value of your home. But you do not make any repayments of interest or of the capital. Instead, the interest on the loan is added to your debt each year. So year by year your debt grows, and when you finally die your home is sold and the debt is repaid. The interest charged on a lifetime mortgage is about 7 per cent, rather more than the best deals you can get with a regular mortgage. The companies say that is because it can be many years before the debt or the interest will be paid. But that is nonsense. They just know there is not much competition and they charge accordingly.

The real problem with lifetime mortgages is that you get relatively little but it can end up eating up the whole value of your home. For example, if you are 70 and your home is worth £200,000 you can borrow about a quarter of that amount – £50,000. If you live 20 years, at 7 per cent that debt will have grown to almost £200,000 by the time you die. Of course, the value of your home may also have grown – but you cannot guarantee that. So it is possible that having £50,000 now will cost the entire value of your property. Now you may not mind about that – and if you have children they may not care either. But it does mean you cannot know how much of the value of your home will be left for your heirs when you die. It is safest to assume it will be nothing.

In the past there was a danger that the debt would exceed the value of your home and you could be forced to leave the home to repay the debt. Nowadays that should not happen. You should only ever consider a scheme that guarantees your debt can never exceed the value of your property and you are safe to stay there all your life, if you want.

You can reduce the cost of these schemes by taking what is called a 'drawdown' plan. You still arrange to borrow, say, £50,000. But instead of taking it all at once you just draw it down when you need it: for example, when the roof needs repairs or when you fancy that world cruise. You are only charged interest on the part of the £50,000 you have actually spent. That way the debt grows much more slowly.

Whatever type you choose there will be fees at the start which will reduce the amount you get.

You may find a company that will do lifetime mortgages (sometime called a 'roll-up loan' or a 'rolled-up interest loan') for someone as young as 55. But at that age you will only be able to borrow at most about 10–12 per cent of the value of your home. You should avoid them until you are at least 65 if you can. Even at that age you can only borrow about 20 per cent of the value of your home. At 75 that rises to about 35 per cent and at 85 it is about 45 per cent. So hang on if you can.

A **home reversion** is the name given to the other type of equity release product. You sell a share of your home to a finance company for a cash sum. You will always get a guarantee that you can live there for as long as you want. Because you do not borrow any money no debt is piling up. But the finance company owns a proportion of your home, and as the value of your home rises so does the value of the company's share. The advantage is that you do at least know what proportion will be yours to leave to your heirs. Also, if you need more money in a few years you can sell another portion of it.

Home reversion schemes cannot normally be found for anyone under 65 and even then there are restrictions on the value of your home. How much you will get will depend on your age and sex – women live longer and therefore get less than men of the same age, and couples get least of all because the company does not get its money until both partners have died or gone into care. For example, a single man aged 70 with a £200,000 home who took a home reversion scheme on half of it might get a lump sum of about £48,000. A single woman would get £44,000 and a couple just £40,000. But in your 50s, forget it.

If you do consider a scheme to raise money on your home, think carefully about what you want the money for. The debt will be with you for the rest of your life. Make sure the advantage lasts that long too. If your home needs urgent repairs it may be better to take out a straightforward second mortgage if you can afford the monthly repayments.

Home Improvement Agencies (also known as Staying Put Agency or Care & Repair) are local charitable organisations that help older or disabled people to repair or improve their homes. They may offer a much better deal than a commercial lender. Search for your local one at www.housingcare.org/search/home-improvement-agency.aspx or contact your local council or social services department.

For further information access the information sheet Equity Release Plans on the website www.helptheaged.org.uk.

EQUITY RELEASE REGULATION

Equity release products are regulated by the Financial Services Authority – but not very well. Research by the FSA found that many people were mis-sold these products. One of the commonest tricks was to encourage people to borrow more than they needed and then sell them an investment product to take up the spare. That way the sales person earned two lots of commission.

Despite stern warnings by the regulator the most recent research shows there are still problems with the mis-selling of equity release. So you should always protect yourself by dealing only with providers and sales companies which belong to a voluntary code called Safe Home Income Plans or SHIP. All sales staff with these companies have a qualification in equity release products. You can download a useful checklist on equity release from www.ship-ltd.org.

USING THE FUNDS RAISED

Most people keep the money in the bank and use it as and when they need it. Alternatively, you can convert the capital into an income for life by buying a purchased life annuity. But in your 50s any company that promises you an income for life has to reckon on paying you for a very long time.

So if you raised even £100,000 from your home one way or another, a single woman aged 55 would get an income about £418 a month for life. A man would get £435. A couple would get rather less than either between them. Non-taxpayers would get slightly more. Younger people would get less, older ones would get more. For more about purchased life annuities see pages 110–12.

Any money you do raise from your home will affect how much you can claim through any means-tested benefit such as Income Support, income-based Jobseeker's Allowance, Pension Credit, Housing Benefit, Council Tax Benefit, or Child Benefit or Working Tax Credit. A good adviser will discuss all that with you before you commit yourself. ■

PART II

CUTTING SPENDING

Part I was about boosting your income. Part II is about spending less. If you do both, it's win-win. More income and less spending means more money left over for the really nice things in life – or of course less debt, which is always good. If you find paying off debt a pretty boring thing to do with money, consider the other side of it – the panic of having debt and no way of paying it off.

Some of this part is also about what to do with that surplus income – things that on the face of it are pretty boring, like paying off debt. But if you have ever wondered why there are so many rich people in banking it is because not finding all that stuff boring can make you a lot better off.

So by combining part I and part II you come up with a magic potion to leave you better off and dispel those terrible clouds of anxiety that money – especially lack of it – can bring.

8

REDUCING EXPENDITURE

REDUCING EXPENDITURE

How often have you looked in your purse or pocket, found a few coins and a crumpled fiver and thought, 'I only got that out on Tuesday. Where does it go?' Despite the rise of plastic we are still addicted to cash – bits of metal and paper that have been used as money for nearly three thousand years (the metal, at least – paper is a bit more modern). Technology has helped fuel this addiction rather than reduce it. Cash machines are back doors into our own bank accounts and through them our money is draining away. Over the year we make 2,750,000,000 visits to cash machines and take out £180,000,000,000 in tenners and twenties. The average withdrawal is £65 but in just five days we are back asking for more. Add on the cash we get from other places and this means that for each of the 365 days a year every adult is spending a £20 note.

KEEPING TRACK OF MONEY

Just where does it go? There is one way to find out. Take slimming diets. There are all sorts of reasons why diets don't work. But one technique for eating less (and hence losing weight) that does work is to keep a diary of everything you eat. Just the fact you are going to have to write it down can be enough to keep that biscuit, sweet or glass of wine out of your mouth.

It is the same with money. Write down everything you spend, not at the end of the day as you might with a normal diary, but when you spend it (or shortly after if you would find it too embarrassing to make a note in the newsagent, the coffee shop, the department store, the garage, the sandwich bar or the pub). You will be surprised. It is very easy with cash to rack up not just the average £20 a day but £30, £40 or more. When you know where it went you can start cutting things out. It can make a big difference.

For example, if you spend £3.10 on a cappuccino and croissant on your way to work every day, how much will that cost you over the year? There are about 225 working days in the year so you might guess about £700 a year; that is probably rather more than you expected, so it might make you want to check the calculation. But in fact it costs a lot more than that. Breakfast is bought out of your taxed income. If you work you pay 20 per cent tax and 11 per cent National Insurance contributions, which is a total of 31 per cent tax. So to have £697 to buy your *petit déjeuner* you have to have earned £1,011. Giving it up would be the equivalent of a £1,000 pay rise. It is enough to make you choke on your Danish. In fact, every £1 you spend every working day – whether on a bus fare, a newspaper, a coffee, a bar of chocolate, a magazine or a bottle of water (so that's where it went!) is the equivalent of taking £326 off your annual pay.

What do you notice about all those things? What they have in common is that they will not last any longer than the day you bought them. In other words, they are not necessary – especially the water: the healthiest water in fact comes out of a tap, free, and it is a myth – believed more by young people than those in their 50s – that we need to drink water so frequently that we have to carry it round like camels.

So by cutting down a bit on the little things you spend every day you can make a big difference to your income by the end of the year. If your boss called you in and offered you a pay rise of £1,000 a year, would you turn it down? No. This is just the same.

That might have felt like a bit of a lecture – give up the nice things and, guess what, you will be better off. So next we will look at the horrid things that we can get rid of with a bit of effort and, let's hope, save even more.

CASH

The first stop is that cash machine. Most cash machines are good. They let you take your money out of your own bank account without charging you. That applies to every machine on bank or building society premises (including those facing the street outside) and almost every machine run by a bank or building society. But there are other machines that are still in the Link network, and sometimes even have the word 'free' somewhere on them, that charge you to take out money (the word 'free' only applies to checking your balance). These are run by private companies and you will find them in shops, garages, motorway service stations, pubs, clubs and even some post offices. They will charge you between £1.25 and £2.50 to get cash, which is a lot to pay if you are only taking out a tenner. Under the rules – which they sometimes obey as minimally as they dare – they have to tell you on the screen or on the machine itself whether a charge will be made. Just before you get your money you have to press a button to agree to the charge. Always avoid these machines.

You can find your nearest cash machine and whether it charges or not at www.link.co.uk. Make a note of the nearest free ones and use those. Cash-back from a supermarket or shop is another good way to get cash free of charge. It only works with debit cards and the shop gets the advantage that it has less cash to handle, which is costly for them.

Taking money out of free cash machines can also cost you money if you use the wrong card. Debit cards give you free cash; credit cards do not – they charge you. (For more on the iniquities of credit cards, see chapter 9.) When you take out cash you will pay three times:

- a fee, usually about £3, but if you take out more than £100 it will be more than that
- interest at a special high rate – anything up to 28 per cent
- interest that will start at once even if you pay off your bill in full at the end of the month.

The result is that taking out £100 cash on your credit card can cost you more than £7, even if you pay the bill as soon as it arrives.

If you use any card abroad to take out foreign cash you will pay even more. In addition to the charges in the UK you will also be charged 2.95 per cent 'foreign usage loading'. That applies to debit cards as well as credit cards. So taking out £100 of euro on a credit card in France could cost more than a tenner. Only Nationwide and the Post Office do not make this charge on their cards anywhere in the world; Saga does not charge in Europe but charges 1 per cent elsewhere.

INSURANCE

Meet an insurance person and within three minutes they will have answered any sceptical remark you may make about their livelihood with the well-worn phrase 'insurance is sold not bought'. They mean that we have to be persuaded to do something as sensible as buy insurance. But in fact not buying insurance can be a very sensible decision – because often it is not worth having. However, it might still be sold to you. Or rather you might be sold 'protection' because that is the new brand for insurance that the industry promotes. So looking at insurance and avoiding it wherever possible is a very good way of keeping more money to spend on important things – such as savings, pensions and holidays.

Even though insurance doesn't protect us from anything, it does provide compensation if something bad happens – sometimes. If car insurance protected us from accidents or life insurance protected us from death, it would be a much better buy.

LIFE INSURANCE

Every year the insurance industry comes up with a specious figure it calls the 'protection gap' – the amount of insurance we actually have deducted from the amount of insurance it says we ought to have. The figure is huge – in the billions. But in fact it is quite possible that we have far too much life insurance. One reason is that life insurance is not just sold, it is sold secretly. We accumulate life insurance policies that are bundled willy-nilly with our pension, our endowment, our mortgage, our loans, or with other insurance against illness or unemployment.

Of course, there are circumstances in which life insurance is a vital, valuable and, at its best, cheap product. If you have people who are financially dependent on you, you will want to make sure as far as you can that your unexpected death will not leave them with financial problems. However, the objective of insurance sales people is not to protect us, but to earn easy commission.

So question 1 is 'Do you need life insurance at all?'. If you have no dependants the answer is simply 'no'. A single person who is not a parent and who does not have a joint mortgage with anyone does not need life insurance. That does not stop the industry trying to sell it – even suggesting falsely that if you die without life insurance your relatives would have to pay your debts. (Note: when you die the value of your estate is added up – property, possessions, savings and so on – and your debts are paid from that. If your debts are more than your estate, no one has to pay the balance. Some people might call that a result.)

If you have dependants, question 2 is 'What will they need if I die?'. Children are the first consideration. In this case, you probably need what is called 'term assurance', a cheap product that replaces your income until your youngest child is independent – say, 21. Then it comes to an end. Next, your spouse or partner: nowadays, husbands and wives lead more independent financial lives than they used to and penury does not always follow the death of one partner. But if one partner is dependent on the other modest life assurance can make sure that joint debts can be paid and funeral expenses met.

There is one thing that definitely needs protecting: your home. If you have a joint mortgage – one that is in your name and someone else's – it is important to make sure that if one of you dies before it is paid off life insurance repays the debt in full, otherwise the survivor may face the prospect of having to sell the property to repay the loan. If you have an endowment mortgage, the amount you pay each month will already include life insurance to repay the loan if one of you dies. Many people with a repayment mortgage will also have been sold life insurance when they took it out.

Beyond that is up to you and your dependants to decide. But before paying for a policy ask what insurance you already have. If you belong to a company pension scheme you probably have life insurance already, often as much as three times your annual salary. That may well be enough.

The unnecessary sale of life cover comes back to commission – the sales agent can get more than two years' premiums up front and 2.5 per cent of your annual premiums for the rest of your life. So cancel any life insurance policies that you do not really need.

OTHER TYPES OF INSURANCE

Life insurance is not sold in isolation. Muggers usually work in pairs. Once you have agreed to cover your life you will often be told that there is more chance of serious illness or disability than of death – which, if you think about it for a moment, is clearly nonsense. Guess what? They have just the policy to cover you for that.

Typically, **critical illness cover** will cost you about £30 a month and will promise £100,000 if you get one of seven major health problems – such as cancer or heart disease. It sounds useful. But the criteria for claiming are becoming stricter and stricter. Some cancers are now excluded and some companies will pay out only after your second heart bypass operation. All the while, premiums are rising rapidly. In other words, take it out now and by the time you may need it you may find the growing premiums you have paid, perhaps for years, were a waste of money. Do not buy it. If you have, think about cancelling.

In 2006 the Financial Services Authority found widespread problems with the sales process for critical illness insurance and the information given to customers. Again, blame commission. The salesperson can keep up to half your premiums for up to four years. That may earn them £2,000 for one sale.

A better deal for younger people – and that is why it pays much less commission, because there is much less profit to pay it from – is called permanent health insurance or PHI. It pays out if disability or illness prevents you from working, which is much more likely than getting one of the 'dread diseases' that critical illness policies insure against. PHI replaces up to 75 per cent of your income, though some insurers are now reducing this to 60 per cent. But policies will not pay out beyond a certain age – sometimes as young as 50. Remember that in the event of illness or disability many employers will keep you on full pay for six months and on half pay for a further six months. There is no point in paying for cover when your employer will pay up anyway. Some policies will only pay up if you are incapable of doing any work, not just your normal job, which is a tough condition to meet. The premiums will get more expensive as you get older.

Another insurance to consider ditching is **private health cover**. In the UK health care is free. Or rather, we have all paid for it through our taxes. So your premiums are buying you not full health care but the difference between what the NHS will provide and what your private insurance will give you. If you have an acute medical problem, the chances are that the same people will look after you and the same surgeon will operate, often no more quickly and sometimes in the same theatre. So all you are buying is a shorter wait for non-urgent treatment, a private room, and perhaps a sense of being more important than the hoi-polloi. Such things have a price – but generally not the high cost of private health care insurance.

As you get older those premiums will rise. So when you reach the age when treatment becomes more likely, you may find you cannot afford to pay the charges.

It is better to put the money you would have spent on the premiums into a separate savings account which you reserve for your health. If you need treatment for a painful but non-urgent condition or you want to speed up tests for something you think might be dangerous but which your GP will not call urgent, use that money to buy private care. Many hospitals offer guaranteed prices on common operations. Leave the NHS to take care of the rest.

Payment protection insurance is another money-spinner. It will always be offered to you when you take out a loan, a credit card, or a mortgage. It is normally sold as 'protecting your payments if you fall ill or lose your job' – which is not true. These products do not pay out in many circumstances, including being over pension age or losing your job due to anything other than compulsory redundancy. Many do not cover all your payments for the length of the loan.

Research by the Financial Services Authority in 2007 found that these exclusions were not made clear in half the sales they examined. Less than a third of clients were asked about their health – which can affect whether a claim is paid – and most sales staff omitted other key information. Payment protection cover can double the cost of a bank loan. The only people who get peace of mind from them are those who sell them – they get a guaranteed cut as long as you pay the premiums. If you really, really want it, get it online from an independent broker. It can cost as little as a tenth of what it would cost to buy it from the bank which is lending the money.

Extended warranties are deceitful even in their name. They are simply an insurance policy that covers the cost of repairs if an electrical item stops working properly. They are never worth having. But commission rates drive the market – the people who sell the product will earn as much again or more if they sell you this insurance as well. Unlike most insurance these sales are unregulated and usually made by people who know little about it. All goods sold retail are covered by laws which guarantee them for a year. Some stores guarantee their goods for longer. Research by the Consumers' Association shows that extended warranties are generally a waste of money, because modern appliances are very reliable and are unlikely to break down within five years.

Equally bad is **credit card protection**. If your cards are lost or stolen you are not liable for anything bought on them as long as you took reasonable care and you tell the card company swiftly. So you are being asked to pay to insure the risk taken by the credit card provider. Also, if you are paying out for a service to register all your cards in case they are stolen, that is a complete waste of money. You can call and tell the card company yourself. Calls of that sort are nearly always free.

Cancelling insurance can be a very good way to save money, as well as to bask in the warm glow that you are paying less to banks and insurance companies for useless products.

TAKE POWER

About half the UK population has never switched their gas or electricity supply from the days when the choice was limited to one national gas supplier and the local electricity board. For many, that is money down the drain. Another half – probably overlapping hugely with the first group – still pay their gas and electricity bills by cash or cheque when they get the quarterly bill. That is more money down the drain. Probably another half – at a guess, as there are no official figures – have not taken any steps to insulate their home or make it energy-efficient. That is still more money down the drain. So let's unblock those drains and recover those missing fivers.

Would you like to save £80 a year? It's easy. Get out your electricity and gas bill, call the supplier and say you want to pay by monthly direct debit in future. Your energy costs will fall by up to £80 a year. It is not a free lunch. Your bill will still be worked out every quarter – it is the way they have always done it and why fix something that is not broke? But the direct debit will be taken every month, which means the energy company will not know how much to charge you. So it will make an estimate and charge you that. Corporate nature being what it is, the estimate will err on the side of taking too much rather than too little and it will not pay you any interest on the excess. But you can get the excess back at the end of the year if you ask for it. Check over a year to see whether the payments roughly balance the cost.

While you are doing this why not look for a cheaper supplier? If you have never changed your supplier – and half of us have not – there is bound to be one. Even if you have changed there will probably be one. That could save you another £120 a year (we are talking free lunches for a week or more now). This time there is no catch, as long as you do it the right way. If someone comes to the door, calls you on the phone or sends you an email telling you how much you can save by switching, ignore them. They are sales people and their advice is neither impartial nor trustworthy. Instead, go to one of the dozen or so websites that are licensed to operate services to let you find the cheapest tariff and change to it. You can find a list of them at www.energywatch.org.uk. Type that in carefully because there are commercial sites with similar names waiting to pounce on you to sell you stuff. In fact, you could type in the full page address www.energy watch.org.uk/help_and_advice/saving_money/price_comparison_services/in dex.asp to make sure you get to the right place. At some point in

2008 Energywatch will cease to exist, in which case you may be redirected to the website of the National Consumer Council, www.ncc.org.uk.

These licensed services are not charities – they make up to £60 every time someone changes supplier so they are very keen to promote the benefits of changing. Also, note that the best time to change may not be right now. The price of gas and electricity goes up and – sometimes – down quite frequently, but the six major suppliers do not alter their tariffs at the same time. So there is little point in changing until all of them have a bit of a pause after a round of price changes.

A helpful website keeps track of this time and with a simple traffic light signal says 'go for it' or 'stop and wait' (or sometimes amber when the decision is more finely balanced). It is www.moneysavingexpert.com and it has links to the online services which let you do the change. If you go through moneysavingexpert you might even get a better deal such as cash-back or free wine.

Switching supplier is simple and happens quite quickly. Just to put your mind at rest, the same gas and the same electricity comes through the same pipes and cables. It is just the bill that comes from a different place.

You can also shop around for boiler servicing.

Every home in the UK (just about) is on the electricity network. But not everyone is connected to piped gas. About 15 per cent have to rely on oil or liquefied petroleum gas (LPG) delivered by lorry. Those prices have gone up too but there is very little competition and very little you can do to save money. The Competition Commission has looked into the LPG situation and more competition should be coming into the market in 2008. So check what is available and with luck you could save some money there too.

ENERGY-SAVING

Paying by direct debit and changing supplier (if you can) will save you money. But what about the environment? Cheaper fuel is good as long as having it does not encourage you to waste even more of it (yes, even more of it – because we all waste it).

Fortunately, the cheapest and easiest things save the most. Forget about wind turbines in the back garden, solar panels on the roof or renewing your central heating boiler (modern condensing boilers use far less energy). All three are good but the payback time is very long so it is not worth considering them unless you intend to stay in your home for a good few years. But draughtproofing your external doors (and cat-flap) and your windows, insulating the loft with 270 millimetres (10½ inches) of the fluffy material, and lagging your hot water tank and pipes are all much cheaper. They will also pay back the outlay within a few years. Switching to energy-saving light bulbs is another way to save energy at low cost. The Government plans to phase out incandescent bulbs by 2011.

Cavity wall insulation is another good bet if your home has cavity walls. These became common from the 1940s and were not routinely insulated until the 1970s (and not compulsorily so until the 1990s). You can even insulate solid walls on earlier homes, though it may not look very pretty and might reduce the size of your rooms. Fitting double glazing is good but costs a lot of money so the payback can be many years. For more information see the Energy Saving Trust website at www.energysavingtrust.org.uk; also, look for the Trust's 'Energy Saving Recommended' label on some products.

There are other things you can do to save money and energy that involve no expense at all. First, whenever you buy electrical equipment such as a fridge, a washing machine or a dishwasher, make sure it has a label stating that its energy usage is 'A' (some modern refrigerators are so efficient that the scale goes up to A++). They use the least power and that will save you money.

No similar system applies to televisions, DVDs, satellite boxes, CDs, music centres or other audio equipment. So it is much harder to find out in the shop or online how much they will use (a) when they are on and (b) when they are on standby. But if you are buying a new TV an LCD flatscreen uses less power than a plasma. Also, note that the Energy Saving Trust puts recommended products on its website.

COST AND PAYBACK OF ENERGY-SAVING MEASURES

Action	Annual saving (£)	Cost (£)	Payback (years)
Energy-saving bulb (each)	7	3	0.4
Hot water tank jacket	20	12	0.6
Pipe insulation	10	10	1.0
Floor insulation	60	110	1.8
Insulate uninsulated loft	110	500	4.5
Cavity wall insulation	90	500	5.6
Solid wall insulation	300	1,900	6.3
Draughtproofing	20	200	10.0
Topping up 50mm loft insulation to 270mm	30	500	16.7

Source: Energy Saving Trust www.energysavingtrust.org.uk

It is almost impossible to find out whether turning audiovisual equipment off at the mains will mean you have to reset tuners and clocks. But if you can turn it off that is what you should do. All the time it is on standby, power is draining out of your house, and money out of your bank account. About 10 per cent of our electricity bill is said to come from equipment left on standby. It is best to turn it off at the mains. You can get special power sockets that respond to remote controls to turn things off completely rather than leaving them on standby and using power.

Another big waste of energy is leaving mobile phones and MP3 players on charge when they are full and leaving chargers plugged into the mains when nothing is being charged. We know they use power then because they are warm: the heat has to come from some-where – and you are paying for it. Computers and printers left on also consume power. Switch them off when you go out and overnight. Turning appliances off can save you £100 a year. ∎

9
DEALING WITH DEBT

DEALING WITH DEBT

Debt can be good. Debt is the way we match the ups and downs of our spending with the fairly constant flow of our income. It is the way to have stuff now when we do not actually have the money – yet. But debt can also be bad. Smoothing out the ups and downs is fine. But spending more than your income cannot last forever. Debt can lead to misery, worry, sleepless nights and, in some extreme cases, death – yes, it has happened. BBC Television's *Panorama* in 2006 claimed that there had been at least 17 debt-related suicides in the previous three years. Debt can also lead to bankruptcy – which might, for some people in some circumstances, be the right answer. But it is never an easy way out.

The trouble is that we are all addicted to debt. As individuals we owe about £220 billion in consumer credit – not including mortgages, which are different for reasons explained later. So we owe about £5,000 for every adult in the country. In other words, we have spent £5,000 more than we have earned. The trouble is that debt is not distributed evenly. Lots of people owe lots of money, while lots of others owe nothing at all.

It is not just individuals who are addicted. The Government is, too. Read what it said at the start of a paper published in 2003 proposing changes in the law governing consumer credit: 'Consumer credit is central to the UK economy.'

The banks are addicted, too. A considerable proportion of the tens of billions of pounds they make in profit comes from lending us money at high rates of interest.

In your 50s debt can creep up on you, especially as your income declines or your expenses rise. Taking on debt can seem easier than reducing your standard of living, and the banks are usually happy to oblige – but it is not a good idea. Debt is double spending – you borrow the money and spend it and then you carry on spending when you pay the interest. And as we get older there is less time to undo the mistakes we make.

GOOD DEBT/BAD DEBT

You might think that good debt is debt you can afford and bad debt is debt you cannot afford. If only it were that simple. Most people who get into debt think they can afford it. No. Good debt is debt you control. Bad debt controls you.

Short-term debts that simply bring spending forward a few months – say, up to a year – can be good debt. We borrow some money, we buy something now, and we pay for it over a fairly short period. But a golden rule of debt is that you should never pay for something over a longer period than you are using it. So if you take two holidays a year, you should not borrow the money to pay for them over more than six months. Do not take on debt at Christmas and still have it hanging around on 25 December next year – and avoid buying clothes on a credit card which you do not pay off until after you have stopped wearing them.

Good debt can also be spreading the cost of something that lasts a long time that you could not buy out of income. Your washing machine packs up. Your car needs replacing. Your daughter says she is getting married. These things are hard to afford without debt and, of course, they have to be paid for now rather than in a few years' time. Those debts can run for a couple of years, maybe three; but if you have to run them much beyond that it probably means you could not afford the item in the first place.

Good debt might also be to help you get that new kitchen, a loft extension or a garage. Improvements to your home last a long time and it is perfectly reasonable to secure the loan on your home. However, that means that if you find you cannot repay the debt your home is at risk. So take care, but bear in mind that home improvements are the one kind of debt that you can secure on your home.

CREDIT CARDS

With those general rules out of the way let us look at the sources of credit starting with the easiest and most flexible of all – credit cards.

It is partly because they are so easy and flexible that credit cards are being used by the banks to take more money off us. Although they made more than £40 billion profit in 2006 the banks are under pressure and we are all in line to help them out. So credit cards are getting more expensive and more complicated almost by the day.

Many people, even those over 50, do not understand the tricks that credit cards use to part us from our cash.

The interest-free trick Most people think that interest is not charged for the first 56 days on stuff bought with a credit card. Wrong! Wrong! Wrong!

- You only get any interest-free period if you pay off your bill in full within the deadline stated. If you do not pay it off in full, interest is charged from the moment of purchase.
- If you *do* pay your credit card bill in full you only get interest-free credit from the day of purchase until you pay it off. So that is a maximum of 56 days. Hence, things you bought on the first day of the monthly statement have 56 days' free credit. Things you bought on the last day of the statement have 25 days' free credit.
- Not all credit cards have 56 days' free credit. Some have as little as 46. Also, some that say they have 56 actually have a shorter period of 46 days for – you've guessed it – the people who regularly pay off in full.

The APR trick 1 A card that advertises 16.9 per cent APR has to charge you 16.9 per cent interest. Wrong! To advertise a particular APR (annual percentage rate) the bank has to give that rate to two out of three customers. The others can be charged anything at all – 27.9 per cent if it likes. Customers with a good credit rating will get 16.9 per cent. Those with a slightly worse rating could be charged more.

The APR trick 2 A bank that says it will charge you 16.9 per cent cannot, by law, charge you more. Wrong! Wrong!

- The APR is rounded to the nearest one decimal place. And guess what? Nearly all banks charge you the most they can, which rounds down to the advertised rate. So 16.9 per cent is normally 16.945 per cent, which conveniently works out to 1.313 per cent per month. OK, 0.045 per cent is not going to cost you much over a year – it is 87p a year on a £1,000 debt. But if you reckon the total credit card debt is about £55 billion that will make the banks collectively some £50 million a year.
- The APR quoted is for items you purchase using the card. If you use the card to get out cash the APR will be more. A lot more. Always more than 20% often close on 30%. And as a footnote see the next trick.

Credit card cheque trick Using a credit card cheque is just like using a credit card. Wrong! Credit card cheques are sent out automatically by some banks to their credit card customers. You can use them in a shop to buy things or to pay a bill by post. But they count as cash. So interest is at a higher rate – often nearly 30 per cent – and straight away, because there is no interest-free period with cash (see page 147).

The order of payments trick When you make a payment the money is used to pay off the most expensive bit of the loan first. Wrong! In fact, completely the opposite is the case. As we have seen, on one card you can have debts at different rates of interest. Almost all card companies use the payment you make to repay the least expensive debt first, leaving the most expensive one hanging around for years.

The minimum payment trick Paying off the minimum each month is the best way to keep your credit card under control. Wrong! Wrong! Wrong! This cannot be over-emphasised. *If you pay off only the minimum each month you will be in debt for years.* Just how many years will probably surprise you.

The minimum payment the card company asks for is cunningly fixed to make your debt stretch into the distant future. Suppose you owe £1,000 on your credit card and the rate of interest you pay is 16.9 per cent APR. You pay off the monthly minimum used by many cards – 2 per cent of the debt or £5 if that is more. Then it will be a staggering 23 years before it is repaid. Over that time you will have paid £1,545 in interest – more than you borrowed in the first place.

The answer is simple – *don't pay just the minimum*. Take your current payment – say it is £20.26 a month – and make a standing order to repay that much each month. If you can afford it now you can afford it in future. Do that and your debt will be cleared in six years and nine months and you will pay just £626 in interest, a saving of £918.

If you are horrified that, even after that big effort, a debt of £1,000 would still take more than six years to clear, then double your repayment to £40.52. Then it will be gone in just two years seven months and cost £221.48 in interest, saving you more than £1,300. Even better, you have stopped the bank taking more than £1,300 off you for nothing.

Remember, banks are clever at sums. Customers on the whole are not. This is why the banks turn in record profits year after year – while we are a bit hard up, most of the time.

HOW TO WIN AT CARDS

Like most aspects of personal finance, credit cards should be simple. You buy things with the card. The amount you pay is lent to you by the credit card company (let us call it 'the bank', to make life easier, even though sometimes it is not a bank). The bank charges interest on that amount from the day you spend it. The bank sends you a statement once a month. It asks you to pay a minimum amount – usually 2 per cent of the total (or £5 if that is more). You can of course pay more than that – if you want to, you can pay off the whole lot. If you pay your whole bill off in full by the date it says the interest is waived. Otherwise it is not. If you miss the payment date you are fined £12. If you use the card to spend more than your credit limit you are fined £12.

People often ask 'What's the best credit card?' and the only correct answer is another question: 'What do you want to use it for?' Before considering that, here are some basics.

Cards are normally sold on the APR – the annual interest rate charged on the debt. APRs have been creeping up and range from 6.8 per cent to, believe it or not, 41.2 per cent. The average is about 16.9 per cent. So if you have a debt of £1,000 at an APR of 16.9 per cent you will have to pay £169 a year – £3.25 every week – in interest alone. It is your rent for the £1,000. So at the end of year, even though you have paid £169, you will still owe £1,000.

In fact it is not quite that simple. The way APR is calculated allows banks to work it out in a dozen different ways. Some charge from the moment the goods are bought. Others are quicker to charge interest on the interest owed. *So one card may cost you more than another even if they have the same APR.* However, a card with a higher APR will normally be more expensive to borrow on than one with a lower APR. So it remains a good guide. The banks are looking into how to make the APR easier to understand. Don't hold your breath.

If you do not use the card to borrow, i.e. if you pay it off in full every month, you will normally not pay any interest, so the APR is irrelevant. Instead, look for cash-back and as long an interest-free period as possible – 58 days can be found.

Here is a classification of credit cards – or rather, credit card users.

You pay off your card in full every month without fail.
Two out of three people pay off their cards in full every month or nearly every month. If you are in the 'nearly' group, ignore this tip and go straight to the next one. If you are genuinely in the always always always group – which is 58 per cent of the credit card holders in the UK – note this tip.

Some credit cards will give you money every time you use your card. It is called cash-back and the best long-term deals are 1 per cent – so for every £1,000 you spend on the card you get back a tenner. Now you may think that you do not spend anything like that on your credit card. But why not? If you are paying it off in full every month there is no reason why you should not pay for everything on it – from groceries to newspapers, from petrol to a box of chocolates. Now of course you have to be careful and you have to put aside the money you need to pay that bill at the end of the month. Do not look at your bank balance and think 'that looks healthy' and spend more on clothes or that weekend away. But with discipline you can use cash-back to take money off the banks.

In case you are now feeling sorry for the banks, fear not – they do not lose much at all. In fact, they will normally lose hardly anything. Every time you use your credit card the card issuer takes a small fee from the amount you pay. With Visa or Mastercard it is not quite 1 per cent, though with American Express it is rather more. So in fact you are just getting back what the retailer is paying. Also, some cards put a limit on how much cash-back you can get or drop the rate after you have spent a certain amount.

But some cards pay you a lot more in the first three months. Like all deals these are likely to be changed by the time you read this but at the start of 2008 you could get 4 per cent on all spending for three months from Capital One and 5 per cent on up to £4,000 spending from American Express Platinum card. If you do decide to go for a cash-back card, read the terms and conditions carefully to make sure you understand what the cash-back is and how it will be paid to you. And *never* miss paying your bill in full. If you do, the chances are that the interest the bank earns on that one month's borrowing will be bigger than the whole of the cash-back saving you make in a year. So call the card company and tell it you want to pay by direct debit and you want to pay the bill off in full.

You may be tempted by cards that offer rewards or air miles or give money to charity. Forget them. Occasionally one out-performs cash-back – but not often. If you want to give to charity use a cash-back card and then Gift Aid the money (see box overleaf).

People who pay off their credit card in full each month can also benefit from the next tip, as an alternative to the cash-back tip – perhaps after the 4 per cent initial period has passed.

You normally pay off your debt in full but occasionally – because of Christmas, summer holidays, a friend's wedding – you do let a bit of debt sit there for a month or two.

GIFT AID

Gift Aid is tax relief on money donated to UK charities. Any UK taxpayer wishing to make a donation directly to a charity can use Gift Aid to increase the value of their donation. It has no cost implications and will not affect their tax code. The charity can then reclaim the tax from HM Revenue and Customs.

If you are a UK taxpayer and have paid an annual amount of income or Capital Gains Tax at least equal to the amount of tax being reclaimed by the charity, you can apply to be a Gift Aid donor. The Gift Aid Donor Declaration form asks for your name, address, the name of the charity, type of donation (Gift Aid) and confirmation that you have paid UK tax, to cover the tax the charity will reclaim.

For more details see www.hmrc.gov.uk/charities/gift-aid.htm

This is still sensible borrowing – good debt – but while that debt is there you are paying interest on it and rates have been going up recently. Here is how to avoid it – and still make some money.

Step 1 Search the 'best buy' websites for credit cards that offer the longest period of 0 per cent interest on **spending**. You should be able to get at least 12 months, but these deals come and go.

Step 2 Apply. You will need a good credit rating. Arrange to pay the minimum by direct debit each month. Do that when you apply, if you can (not all cards let you), or ring up as soon as the card arrives

Step 3 **Work out how much you can afford to repay each month until the free credit comes to an end.** Multiply that by the number of months at zero per cent and – here is where you must be disciplined – **that is your spending limit.**

Step 4 Use the card for any spending you would normally put on your card and not pay off in full – perhaps Christmas, that new outfit, a GPS unit – **but only within your overall spending limit.**

Step 5 Every month put the monthly payment from step 3 into a high-interest savings account − check the online 'best buy' sites and aim for more than 6 per cent.

Step 6 When you reach the limit from step 3, **stop spending and cut up the card.**

Step 7 Note in your diary when the 0 per cent deal comes to an end and make a note a month before it. On that date call the card company and find out when you have to pay off the account before you are charged interest.

Step 8 Allow for the slowness of the banking system and take enough money out of your savings account in good time. Pay off the credit card in full. **Cancel the card.** Leave any surplus in your savings account.

You want to pay off your debt in full but you have not been able to for a while and you really want to control it.

In their desperation to get hold of our business the banks come up with ever more eye-catching offers. A few years ago they invented the zero per cent balance transfer. In other words, they would not only welcome you as a new customer, they would welcome your debt too. And − you know what? − they would not charge you any interest at all on the balance for several months. Yes. Zero per cent. It was a welcome pack − a free chocolate on the pillow and a half-bottle of champagne in the mini-bar just to say 'Hi'.

Of course, the banks expected to make money out of you even with an offer like this. They are more all-brain than all-heart. They do this using several cunning little tricks. So the important thing is to take the bait but avoid the hook. Eat the sprat, but do not end up as the mackerel.

It was such a good offer that people who really had very little debt started using it to stooze. They used the offer to borrow money at 0 per cent and then put it in a high-interest account to earn money. But that is not you − at least not yet.

Anyway, to stop the stoozers the banks made zero per cent a bit less attractive. It was still *called* zero per cent. But it was not really zero per cent, because they added a charge which began at 2 per cent of the balance transferred and is now normally about 3 per cent, though you may find a lower one.

But if you have an almost manageable but stubborn debt you can still use 'zero' per cent balance transfer to sort it out cheaply.

First, of course, you must take out the 0 per cent on balance transfers credit card. If you can find one for at least a year without a transfer fee, take it. But generally, go for the longest time you can find. For example, a fee of 3 per cent for a zero per cent that lasts 15 months is an APR of 2.4 per cent, so it is better than a fee of 2.5 per cent for one which only lasts for 12 months. Transfer your current balance – or balances if you want to put all your debt together. Remember, the bank will add the transfer fee, probably 3 per cent, so if you owed £5,000 you will have a debt of £5,150.

Cut up the card. This is very important because you must never, ever use this card. That includes never using it for purchases. It can be tempting because the banks may also offer zero per cent for them too. But remember, you are trying to control your debt, not increase it. And if the zero per cent on purchases ends before the zero per cent for transfers you will be paying interest on those purchases in full because money you pay in will be used to pay off your transferred debt, not your new purchases. So the only thing you are allowed to apply to your new card is a sharp pair of scissors.

Then work out what you can afford to pay each month off the debt. Use the highest one you can really afford. Make sure it is more than the minimum payment and then call the card company and say you want to pay that much each month. Ignore any objections and stick with it.

Open your diary or calendar and find the date when the zero per cent deal comes to an end. Turn back two months and mark in big red letters that you must do something now about moving the debt again. When that date comes, do it. Then repeat the process with a new zero per cent card.

That way you can keep your debt hanging around until it is paid off and paying a very low rate of interest – not zero per cent, but at least just the balance transfer percent.

You never pay off your debt in full and, if anything, it is growing.
If this is you, your credit card debt has definitely moved from good to bad and threatens to take over your life. So you need to take it one step at a time. It will be easier than you think.

Step 1 Write down all your credit cards, the annual interest rates (APR) you pay on each, and how much you owe on each. If you do not know what rate you are paying that is, of course, part of the problem. Another part is that many credit card companies still do not put the APR on your monthly statement. Instead they put the monthly interest rate they charge you. There is no easy way to convert one into the other – unless you find APR = $(1+M)^{12} - 1$ easy (M being the monthly percentage interest rate). So you cannot just multiply by 12. Ring the helpline to find out. That number at least will be on the statement.

Step 2 Sort your cards so that the highest interest rate (APR) is top. Cut that card up (ouch) and go to step 3.

Step 3 Change your payments. Stop paying the minimum, which will leave you in debt for years – possibly for the rest of your life. Instead, decide to pay whatever you are paying now for as long as it takes to clear the debt. If you can, decide to pay twice what you are paying now (see page 149 above for what a difference that makes). Ring the helpline and say you want to change your monthly payments from the minimum to a fixed amount of whatever it is. The operator will try to dissuade you. Ignore them.

Step 4 Check your next couple of statements. When your monthly statement arrives, make sure the payment you have set up is more than the minimum. If you have spent a lot in the month before you cut up the card it may not be. Either send a cheque to cover the difference or ring up again and change it to something bigger.

If you can do this with all your cards, so much the better. In future, just use your debit card for spending and never go overdrawn.

ANOTHER WAY TO CUT CREDIT CARD DEBT

There is an alternative solution if your payment record is good and you can get another card easily enough. The banks are so desperate for each other's business they will even take on new customers together with their existing debt. And some cards will offer you a special low rate of interest on that debt. In other words until you clear the debt it will only be charged at, say, 6.9 per cent instead of the more usual 16.9 per cent. This is called a life-of-balance transfer rate. Now this is cheap borrowing. Remember, take the bait but avoid the hook – and in this case it is quite simple.

- Take out the new card.
- Transfer the balance from your old card.
- Cut up the card and put the bits in separate waste sacks.
- As in the previous tip, call up and set up a constant monthly payment equal to your last credit card.
- Sit back and wait for the debt to disappear.

SAVING MONEY ON CALLS TO FINANCIAL ORGANISATIONS

Here is a little tip about phoning your bank or credit card company, or any financial firm. They all use a cunning trick to take a bit more off us. When you ring them you are asked to pay more for the call so they get a share of it.

Generally they will use a number beginning with 0870. But they all have freephone numbers too (beginning 0800). Naturally they do not publicise these.

Luckily, the nice people at www.saynoto0870.com do, and you can look up your bank there and find the right 0800 number. It makes listening to Vivaldi's Symphony for Customers on Hold slightly more tolerable.

Remember that calls to 0870, 0845 and 0800 are much cheaper from a BT landline than from a mobile or through other services. Even 0800 calls may cost you money through them.

OK, it might be a bit of a long sit. But just look at the figures. Suppose you owe £5,000 and the average rate you pay on that is 16.9 per cent. Paying the minimum, it will take you more than – wait for it! – 41 years to clear that debt and cost you – wait for it again! – £8,908 in interest. Fixing your monthly payments at the £101.31 you currently pay will cut that to six years nine months. Moving all that debt to a life-of-balance card at 5.8 per cent will cut that time – to four years nine months. Not only that, but if you pay twice the current amount you can be debt-free in two years three months and pay just £338 interest, thus saving yourself over £8,500 (and 38 years' anxiety).

Your debt is always around your credit limit and it is quite hard to meet the monthly payments.
Now is the time to seek help. Before you read any further, if you have debts that are already frightening you, bills arriving that you do not open or credit card debts that are a big fraction of your annual income, you need more help than this book can give you. Go at once to one of three national charities that can help. They will not charge you anything and they will act only in your best interest. They are:

- Consumer Credit Counselling Service: 0800 138 1111, www.cccs.co.uk
- National Debtline: 0808 808 4000, www.nationaldebtline.co.uk
- Citizens Advice: find your nearest office at www.nacab.org.uk or in the local phone book.

That is what to do. Here is what not to do: do not contact any of the organisations that advertise in newspapers or on television with promises of sorting out your debt. They are trying to sell you something and make money out of your difficulties. The charities can sort you out for free and they have your interests entirely at heart.

If you are over 60+ and wish to improve your money management skills and confidence generally, as well as getting advice on debt, you could see if a place is available on the 'Your Money

Matters' programme run by Help the Aged and Barclays: see www.helptheaged.org.uk.

GETTING BACK CREDIT CARD FINES

If you exceed your credit card limit or pay your monthly bill late (in other words, you have not followed the advice given above to make sure that you pay at least the minimum by direct debit each month), you will be fined. In the past these fines were often £25 or more every time you broke the rules. But in 2006 the Office of Fair Trading ruled that penalties that high were illegal.

It said that any card provider charging more than £12 would be investigated. So all the card providers cut their penalties to £12. But the effect of the ruling is that anyone who paid more than £12 in the past can get back at least the excess, and usually the whole charge. You can go back six years and if you have thrown away your statements your card provider has to let you have copies of them for a standard payment of £10 – and that is £10 for the lot, not each, as some of them have tried to charge in the past.

Call your credit card company; use the freephone number (see box, page 156) and say you want to reclaim the charges up to 2006. It may be helpful. If not, insist on your rights. Write a letter setting out what you have paid and that you want these illegal charges refunded.

FURTHER ADVICE ON CREDIT CARDS

There are no financial advisers or professionals who will help you with credit card choices. That is because there is no commission involved. But if this chapter has whetted your appetite for PVC – which most cards are made of – you should check out www.moneysaving-expert.com. Founded by Martin Lewis (no relation to the author of this book, they both hasten to add), this often eccentric website has the best and most up-to-date guidance on credit cards, including getting back your overpaid charges.

OTHER LOANS

No other loan is as flexible as a credit card – with one exception: the overdraft.

OVERDRAFTS

The courts are currently considering the hefty charges levied by banks on people unfortunate or careless enough to go overdrawn without permission and will in due course decide whether they are legal or not. Whatever the outcome, some level of charge will be allowed. After all, going overdrawn without permission is taking money that is not yours from the bank. Although it is not quite the same as dashing in wearing a balaclava and demanding cash in a bag, it is worth pointing out that in France and many other countries writing a cheque without having the money to cover it is a crime. But in the UK we have, for some reason, come to expect that if we have a bit of a cashflow problem just before our pay arrives the bank will not mind if we spend a bit of its money to tide us over.

This attitude has, of course, been encouraged by the banks. They just charge us a hefty penalty when we do it. In November 2006 Lloyds TSB changed its overdraft penalties so that someone who went overdrawn by 1p could end up owing £345 in penalties and fees three days later. Those tough terms have been relaxed a little since. All the banks are changing their terms and conditions so that what they used to call penalties are now fees for the service of allowing you to spend their money. But going overdrawn without permission can still be very expensive and it is better not to do it.

Overdrafts can still be a good way to borrow money flexibly. It is money when you need it and you can pay it back as it suits you. Some current accounts allow you to go slightly overdrawn without penalties up to a limit – perhaps £250. If you need more than that you have to ask and the bank will give you a higher limit. Charges for an agreed overdraft vary but can include:

- a fee to arrange the overdraft
- a fee to use the overdraft
- a high rate of interest on the amount overdrawn.

Of course, if you exceed the limit set you will be back in penalty territory. So overdrafts, even arranged ones, can be expensive. If you think you may need one, you should pick a current account which has a reasonable approach to overdrafts: no arrangement fee, no usage fee, and a reasonable rate of interest. And always make sure that you keep within the limit.

BANK LOANS

If you find that an overdraft changes from being a helpful friend in time of need and becomes more of a constant companion, you need to consider a way to put that debt back in its place. One of the ways to do that is a bank loan. These loans are not flexible – you have to repay a fixed amount over a fixed period. That means you know what the repayments will be and how long they will last. Nowadays such loans can be very cheap, but that does not mean the bank will not make money out of it. There are several things to watch out for.

How much You cannot borrow small amounts. You will seldom see a bank loan for less than £1,000. Note that the less you borrow, the higher the rate of interest you will pay. You might pay as little as 6.5 per cent for £10,000 but you will pay twice that rate at least if you want to borrow £1,000. With some banks it will work out cheaper to borrow a bit more if that will take your loan into a cheaper tier of interest. The most you can normally borrow on this kind of loan is £25,000.

How long It is always tempting to borrow money over a longer period than you should. Borrowing over a longer period will keep down the monthly repayments. That is because you are repaying less of the capital you borrowed each month. But do not be fooled. Borrowing money over a longer period makes it more expensive, not less, for the simple reason that you will be paying a lot more interest. Even though the rate of interest charged will be much the same over one, five or even ten years, you will be paying that rate of interest for much longer. So the longer the period you borrow over, the higher the total cost.

That is why the best debt is the one you get rid of quickest. This loan will, inevitably, be to pay for things you have already spent money on and may no longer have. So you do not want the debt hanging around forever. Arrange for it to be repaid over the shortest period you can afford.

Insurance When you are offered a loan you will inevitably be asked to take out insurance to cover the repayments. This is called payment protection insurance, or PPI: turn to page 137 to find out why this is generally a bad idea. This section will just look at the cost. The surprising thing is that PPI often more than doubles the cost of a loan. It does not seem like that, but it is all in the arithmetic – which banks are much better at than most of us are.

Take a loan of £5,000, to be repaid over three years at an interest rate of 6.8 per cent APR. Repayments without insurance are £153.57 a month. With insurance they are £176.28. So insurance adds £22.71 to the monthly cost – which does not seem that much. But almost all the monthly payment is in fact a repayment of the capital. The sum of £5,000 divided by 36 (the number of months) is £138.89, so every month you are paying back that much of what you borrowed. Only £14.68 a month is interest, which is far less than the £22.71 a month cost of the insurance. Over the course of the loan you would pay £528 in interest to borrow the money but £817 for insurance that may not pay out anyway.

That is why the banks are so keen to sell us insurance. For people over 50 in particular it is usually a waste of money. But if you do want it you can get it much more cheaply from an independent broker.

Despite more than three years of research and concern about PPI and how it was sold, early in 2008 the Financial Services Authority fined HFC bank more than £1 million for failings in the way it sold PPI to 163,000 customers. The PPI sold by HFC to most of its customers was a particularly iniquitous sort. Instead of adding the charge each month the £1,200 cost of the policy – which included life cover

– was paid for upfront by increasing the size of the loan. And of course interest was paid on that extra amount, making the total cost of the PPI £2,100 on top of an average loan of £3,150. Despite these high costs HFC sales staff managed to sell PPI with three-quarters of the loans. The record fine was imposed on HFC for failing to ensure it gave its customers suitable advice they could rely on.

SHOP LOANS

Would you go to a cake shop for a car? Probably not. But millions of people go to a shop selling sofas or kitchens and come away with a loan. Borrowing the money to buy something you want should not be an add-on to buying the something-you-want. It should be thought about and looked for with the same care as anything else. Otherwise you could end up with poor value and inflexible terms.

Remember too that cheap finance such as 'four years' free credit and nothing to pay for the first year' has to paid for by someone. That someone is you – through higher prices.

AFTERNOON TV

There is nothing wrong with afternoon TV – except the adverts. Every 15 minutes we are invited to sort out our debt, usually by taking on more.

The offers can seem tempting. You can put all your monthly payments together into one place and cut them to a much more manageable monthly payment. You might wonder how this magic is achieved. First, the debt consolidators stretch your debt over a much longer period. So a loan that might have five years to run or a credit card bill that you hope to repay in a few years can be stretched over 20 or 25 years or, as they like to say, 300 months. As shown earlier, that does reduce the monthly payment. But the payments last a lot longer and you end up paying much more interest. Second, that debt is secured on your home. In other words you are taking out a second mortgage. What is more, if you miss a payment or two your home can be taken from you to repay the money. As the loan is secured on your home the lender is taking very little risk. Also, the interest rate is probably a little lower, so by reducing the rate and stretching the loan over many more years monthly payments that seem unaffordable can suddenly seem much less worrying.

But think about it for a minute. What did you buy with that money in the first place? A holiday. A new coat? Your weekly groceries? And you are taking out a mortgage – a mortgage! – over 20 years to pay for it? It is madness.

The other companies that advertise on afternoon TV – and, for that matter, those that take out small ads at the back of the tabloid newspapers – are the ones that offer to sort out your debts not by consolidating them into one big long-term loan but by negotiating with your creditors and perhaps taking advantage of 'a little-known Government law'. They do two things. First, they might negotiate and get your debts put off or the interest frozen. Or they might not. One thing they will do is charge you a fat fee for trying. Yes, they will per-suade you into taking out more debt to deal with your debt. It is mad. But it is also legal. Or they will try to get you what is called an IVA – an individual voluntary arrangement – and charge the banks a fat fee for doing so. These arrangements are not necessarily a bad thing, but you should never use a commercial company to arrange them.

Here is the simple answer to all of this. Instead of spending tomor-row afternoon watching old soaps, antique hunts, or re-runs of courtroom drama series, contact one of the three organisations on page 157 and get your debt sorted out free.

CREDIT REFERENCE AGENCIES

Nowadays we expect instant credit. We apply for a credit card online and get it in the post a couple of days later. We go to a shop and bor-row the money there and then for that new sofa. Or we take out a store card, tempted by the offer of 10 per cent off that day's shopping.

Those instant decisions are possible only because information about our credit record is held on computers that all lenders have access to. If we have a good credit record, we get instant credit. If not, we don't.

In fact, three companies hold information on almost every one

of us. Whenever we do business that involves borrowing – even applying for a mobile phone on a monthly contract – this information is
checked. These are the 'credit reference agencies' that oil the wheels
of instant credit and easy loans.

A lot of the information these agencies hold is publicly available.
They verify our address using the Electoral Roll, which lists every voter
in the UK. Even though you can now tick a box to prevent marketing
companies getting hold of this information, credit reference agencies
still get the whole list. They match it with information from the courts
throughout the UK as well as the Isle of Man and the Channel Islands
on judgments for debt, bankruptcy orders and individual voluntary
arrangements supervised by the courts.

But there is a lot more information that is not in the public domain
– confidential information about our finances provided by the banks,
building societies, insurance companies and others who subscribe to
their service. This information sets out your debts and how promptly
you pay them. All your credit cards are listed together with the credit
limit, what you owe, and how often your monthly payment was on
time, late, or unpaid. Similar information is collected for all your other
credit arrangements – including mortgages, catalogues, store cards or
car loans. Mobile phones on monthly payment plans sneak into the
system because they in effect lend you the cost of the calls which you
then pay at the end of the month. Telecoms, gas, electricity and water
bills are not listed, for legal reasons – but they are lobbying to have
these restrictions removed.

Since 2007 most banks have provided information on current
account overdrafts, sometimes going back several years. In future the
database will include information about total indebtedness and annual
income as well.

Whenever you apply for a loan, a credit card, a mortgage, a bank
account or anything that involves – or could involve – lending you
money the lender will use this credit data as well as information on
your application form to assess whether to lend you money and, if
so, on what terms.

It will assess whether you have borrowed in the past and how well you have dealt with that debt. Paying the correct amount on time each month is excellent; going bankrupt is terrible. Most of us are somewhere in between. Even applying for lots of loans or credit cards over a short time period – regardless of whether you take them up – is bad, because it may mean that you have suddenly hit a financial problem and you want to borrow your way out of it. Strangest of all, having no loans now or in the past is very bad; you have no credit record, so no one knows if you are a good risk or not.

The lender will use this information to produce a credit score from 0 to 1,000 – the higher the better. Those scores are secret, but for a fee the credit reference agencies will now work out a score for you which will indicate the kind of score a lender will work out. Many of them use software provided by the agencies to work out the score. But lenders will also use other information from your application form.

By now you may be wondering how 350 million active credit records on at least 30 million people are held by three agencies and then passed around hundreds of banks and other lenders without our permission. Are there not laws against that sort of thing? Yes, there are. But every time we take out credit or open a bank account a bit of small print allows the company to share our data in this way. Of course, we can choose not to accept this condition – but if we do, the offer will be withdrawn.

However, the data protection laws do give us the important right to see what the companies hold, and all for a fee fixed by law at £2. Unfortunately, the companies have discovered that they can sell us enhanced versions of this information for a higher price. Also, you will be offered access to your credit records for a fee that varies from £4.99 a month – nearly £60 a year – to twice as much. Often these adverts are more prominent on the three agencies' websites than the free £2 offer. Or the more expensive report is offered 'free' but that offer runs out after 30 days and you are then billed for it unless you cancel. (The credit reference agencies have learned their marketing techniques from the banks.)

The more expensive versions might be useful if you are genuinely afraid of identity theft and the fraud it can support. In particular, they can contact you by email or text message every time there is a change on your credit record. So if you have not caused it that could mean someone has been trying to impersonate you. The credit card company Capital One currently offers a limited version of this service free to its customers. So taking out a Capital One credit card can be a cheap way to get access to it. Otherwise, for most of us £2 is all we need to spend to find out what info the agencies hold. You do not even need to pay £2 to all three because almost all financial institutions share data with all of them. So if you get one record it is likely to tell you what is on all the others. Even if you pay for all three credit records, it will cost you just £6.

There is no 'credit blacklist'. However bad your record, there will always be some company which will lend you money. But it will be at a high price. The industry uses the term 'risk-based pricing'. In other words, the higher risk you seem to be, the higher the price you will be charged. More and more banks use it and what it means is that the answer to a credit request may not be a simple 'yes' or 'no'. If you have a poor credit score and pose a greater risk of not paying your bills on time you may still get the loan or the card – but you will be charged more for it.

If you are refused credit, the lender you applied to is supposed to tell you why. However, very often the reason they give will not explain much. Before applying for other credit you should get a copy of your credit record and study it. If you want to correct information on your record which you believe to be factually wrong you will have to write to the provider of the information – the bank or lender – to get it changed. That can take a long time. Alternatively, you can write to the chief executive of the credit reference agency pointing out the error and warning that if the company continues to publish this untrue and defamatory information you will sue.

If the information is correct but you fear that it will be wrongly interpreted – for example, you admit to missing several payments,

WHY YOU MIGHT BE REFUSED CREDIT

If you are refused credit or are offered it at a higher rate than the one advertised, it could be because your credit record has information on it that puts a lender off. That can be as simple as a number of late or missed payments on any of your accounts.

■ It could be because you have some public information the company does not like – for example, if you have moved frequently in the last six years.

■ If you are not on the Electoral Roll – the register of voters – at your present address or a previous address it will be very difficult for you to get credit.

■ If you, or someone in your name, has applied for credit several times in the recent past, that can lower your score. In some cases your name might be linked to that of someone else who is in financial difficulties.

■ Or you could simply have no credit at all – no mortgage, no credit cards, no loans – which means the record will not show whether you are a good risk or not.

but you were abroad for six months or had just been bereaved or lost your job – you can add to your record a 'Notice of correction'. You can state your case in up to 200 words.

Nowadays, your record should not contain information about anyone else unless you have a genuine financial connection with them – for example, a joint mortgage or bank account. The record of someone with whom you have no financial connection should not affect your credit score. If you are wrongly linked to someone else you can fill in a form to 'disassociate' yourself from them and get your records separated. Records are kept for six years. For a credit deal that means for six years after it ends.

There are firms that advertise in the back of newspapers and elsewhere offering to 'repair' your credit record. None of them can legally do any more than you can do yourself – they will just charge you for doing it. Never use them.

Of course, you may be refused credit due to factors that are nothing to do with your credit score. One thing you will be asked for on the application is your age, or, usually, your date of birth. This is not just curiosity. Partly it is for security – it is a useful check question when you call them up – but partly it is ageism. Until the law is changed, age discrimination is still permitted in the provision of goods and services. All the companies really want to work out is whether you will be able to repay the debt or not. In your 50s that probably will not be an issue. In your 60s they will wonder whether your income will last as long as the debt. In your 70s they will begin to ask if you will last as long as your debt. And in your 80s, unless you have a very big pension, forget it.

The three credit reference agencies are:

- Callcredit: 0113 244 1555 or 0870 060 1414, www.callcredit.co.uk/consumer
- Equifax: 0800 783 9421 or 0845 600 1772, www.equifax.co.uk
- Experian: 0800 656 9000 or 0870 241 6212, www.experian.co.uk.

ID THEFT AND HOW TO AVOID IT

ID theft is now supposed to be one of our biggest fears – especially among people over 50. But many people do not know what it means or what it can cost. It is certainly the fashionable crime of the early 21st century – or the crime it is fashionable to fear.

ID theft happens when a criminal steals enough information to persuade a bank or financial company that they are you. They can then:

- buy something using your credit card details
- buy something using a loan which is in your name
- open an account in your name and use that to borrow money
- directly steal money from one of your accounts.

It all looks very frightening. But notice one thing. They all begin with a thief stealing information and using it to pretend to be you. So we can all go a long way to frustrate ID fraud by making sure no one steals enough information to do that. It is up to all of us to keep our data secure.

The first thing is to buy a shredder – a cross-cut one that shreds things into small pieces about 1 inch long and $\frac{1}{2}$ inch wide. Put into it anything that an ID thief might use. That means anything with a printed name and address on it, including, of course, any letter or circular from your bank if it has your details on it. It includes bills or any items from your gas or water company, not just those with a customer number; in fact, any printed direct mail which has come through the post to you. All of it can be used by a crook to pretend to be you, either in a shop or on the phone. When you throw out old bills, bank statements or credit card bills they must all go through the shredder too.

Even if any single item cannot be used directly to commit fraud, several of them can be used to build up a picture. Just a single item can be used to obtain another piece of information, which can then be used to find out more. A lot of crime has been committed using documents obtained by rifling through rubbish bags or, best of all, recycling bins. If you shred it you can still recycle it. Just put out the shredded bits in a bag.

Next, make sure you are careful with your email. Phishing is big business. It means sending bait by email and waiting for people to bite. If you get any email claiming to be from your bank asking you to 'confirm' your password or details or inviting you to click on a link, ignore it. It is not from your bank, however persuasive it might sound.

Here is a real example claiming to be from Abbey Bank plc. Clue no.1: Abbey is not a plc. It is part of the Spanish group Santander. Also, note the odd use of inverted commas and slightly strange English (though it is perhaps no more strange than the English-like language real banks tend to use when they are writing to their customers):

Dear Valued Customer,

Financial institutions around the world have always been subject to attempts by criminals to try and defraud money from them and their customers…as part of our ingoing commitment to provide the "Best Possible" services and protection to all our Members in year "2008", we are now requiring each member to validate their accounts using our new secure and safe SSL servers. To validate your online banking account click on the link below.

<log In To Online Banking>

This email has being sent to all Abbey Bank Customers, and it is compulsory to follow as failure to verify account details will lead to account suspension.*

To be really safe, you should ignore any email that seems to come from your bank as 99 per cent of them are fakes. Sadly, the banks do not make that 100 per cent. The marketing departments still send out emails inviting you to buy things by clicking through a link. Ignore them, too. If you read something you think might be real and you want to follow it up open your web browser and log on in the normal way. Never put in your personal details, passwords or security information under any other circumstances.

In fact, you should never click on an attachment or a web link in an email from anyone you do not know well. By clicking, you can allow a remote website or attachment to download software on to your computer that can spy on your use of your bank account. In addition, always make sure you have a firewall and security software loaded and keep it up to date.

It may all seem a lot of fuss, but if you were standing by a cash machine would you give a complete stranger your PIN? No. Do you keep your money out of site in a wallet in a pocket or bag? Yes. Online security is just the same. If you do anything other than delete these emails at once it is the computer equivalent of going out and leaving your windows and doors open and then being surprised when you are burgled.

However much we do ourselves, our information will leak out. There have been enough data loss scandals in recent times to prove that. But although ID theft is alarming, time-consuming, inconvenient, and at its worst frustrating and even frightening, ultimately it should not cost you any money. The bank should always bear the loss unless you have been involved in the fraud or have been recklessly careless with your data. That is why insurance against ID theft is unnecessary. The banks bear the loss, so why should you pay a premium to cover it?

If you are really worried — or if your details have been stolen and you want to make sure they are not used — you can put a protection on your credit details. If anyone — including you — asks for credit of any sort in your name, further checks will be done to make sure it is really you that is asking for it. The system is run by CIFAS and costs £14.10 a year. The disadvantage is that any application to take out credit or open a current account could be delayed. For more information see www.cifas.org.uk or contact Equifax, the credit reference agency which operates the system, on 0800 783 9421; or send an email to protective.registrationuk@equifax.com

10

CHECK YOUR MORTGAGE – OR PAY IT OFF

CHECK YOUR MORTGAGE
– OR PAY IT OFF

f any debt is 'good' debt it is your mortgage. That is because you used the money to buy an asset which you can always sell, usually for more than you paid for it. So it is very different from the money you borrow to buy a car, a pair of shoes or a plasma TV. You could find it difficult to sell those in a few years' time – and certainly not for more than a fraction of what you paid. So a mortgage is good debt in almost every case. But that does not mean you can ignore it. Even good debt can be expensive. However, as with everything financial you can usually save money by a bit of thought and a tiny bit of effort.

A mortgage used to be for life – but not any more. More than half the business in mortgages is with people who already have a home and who are not moving. They are re-mortgaging to get a better deal. It is the banks' fault. They are so desperate for new business that they offer new borrowers the best terms and when those terms run out the customers show as much loyalty as the banks and take their business elsewhere.

If you have a mortgage and you have not changed lender for some years it is almost certain you can save money by doing so. But nowadays the arithmetic can be so complicated it usually pays to get help. So step 1 is to find a decent broker.

Mortgage brokers come in all sorts. The sort you need is one who is (a) 'whole of market' – a phrase which means the broker will search the whole of the market – or at least a big and representative chunk of it – to find the best deal for you; (b) national, i.e. deals with clients all over the UK and not that bloke over the kebab shop (OK, he might be fine – but he probably isn't); (c) does not charge you a fee. There is some controversy about (c). Some people will say it does not matter. You will end up paying whether the broker charges you or not. But all brokers do get paid by the lender. So why should they get paid by you as well? Or is that what being a middle-man is all about? Anyway, (c) is probably not quite as important as (a) and (b), and (a) is the most important of all. Someone who is not whole-of-market is not worth even considering. See earlier advice on independent financial advisers on page 96.

Whoever you choose, they will try to sell you more than a mortgage – usually insurance. Be very careful about buying it. Insurance is where most brokers make most of their money. Even those who research the whole of the market for your mortgage will almost certainly be tied to one or two companies when it comes to insurance. If you want insurance, go to an insurance broker or buy it online. You will get a better deal.

MORTGAGE CHOICES

There seems to be a bewildering array of choice when it comes to mortgages. There are literally more than 10,000 to choose from. Humans can only cope with that sort of choice by splitting them up. So here goes.

The two kinds of mortgage are:

- repayment
- interest only.

With a repayment mortgage you pay an amount each month that (a) pays the interest on the loan and (b) repays the amount you have borrowed. So at the end of the mortgage term – usually 25 years, but it can be less as you get older – you owe nothing. You have bought your home. Congratulations.

With an interest-only mortgage your monthly payment just covers the interest on the loan. That means that at the end of the deal you have spent 25 years paying interest but have paid nothing off the capital. So you have no home. Needless to say, interest-only mortgages are cheaper – the monthly payments are less. And with property being so expensive a frighteningly high proportion of new mortgages – about one in five – are interest-only. Of course, anyone sensible will have some plans about how to pay off the loan. But the lender generally will not want to know what that is, so it will be up to you. Once you are in your 50s 'interest only' is generally not a good idea unless you are absolutely sure you will come into some money – a pension lump sum, an inheritance, or a maturing investment that will definitely pay off the debt.

The standard rate of interest you will pay on a mortgage is currently about 7.5 per cent. By the time you read this it may be less – or more. But the important thing to remember is that no one should be paying what is called the standard variable rate (SVR) for their mortgage. The SVR is what the lenders would like to get. It is a nice profitable amount. But they also want new business. So they are prepared to cut that SVR by 2 per cent or more to tempt you in. Here is your choice. After that come the warnings, caveats and watch-out-fors.

Fixed rate These loans guarantee the rate of repayment, so the interest rate is guaranteed at, say, 5 per cent over five years. That means that whatever happens to interest rates in the world outside, your mortgage will cost you a known and fixed amount every month for as long as the deal lasts. Fixes, as people call them, can be a very good idea, especially if your income is fixed and it would be a disaster if rates rose and took your repayments up. But a fix is a gamble. If rates rise, you win. If rates fall, you lose and a fix that seemed a good deal today may seem very expensive in three years' time if rates are cut substantially. While the deal lasts you have to stay with it or you will be charged a penalty, often a substantial one. Fixes can last any period but two or five years is common.

Anything that is not a fixed-rate mortgage is a variable-rate one. But they come in several flavours.

Discounted rate If you want a lower rate of interest but do not want to take the gamble of a fix and it does not matter to you if your repayments go up – or down, for that matter – you can get a rate which is a percentage point or two below the SVR. A discount may be 2 per cent or 2.5 per cent below SVR. Some will be one amount below for, say, 18 months and have a smaller discount for the next 18 months. Discounts can last any period but between one and five years is fairly normal. You may find a slightly longer discount period. Others will be called 'trackers' because they will 'track' the base rate fixed by the Bank of England. As that rises and falls so will your mortgage. But instead of being a percentage below the SVR a tracker will be a percentage above base rate. The advantage is that sometimes SVRs are a bit laggardly in going up, or particularly down, when base rates change. But a tracker has to follow it precisely and quickly.

Capped You are the sort of person who wants it all. You want a discount, of course. But you do not really want to see your payments go through the roof. So you can buy a discounted mortgage that goes down any amount but if it goes up the rise is capped. Of course, you pay a bit more for this. In effect, you are paying a bit extra to insure against a big rise in interest rates. Capped rates too can last from one year to a few years.

Others You will come across subtler and more cunning ways to tempt you in. But most will be a variant on or combination of one of the deals above.

WARNINGS ON MORTGAGE OPTIONS

All these deals last for a fixed length of time. If you end one before that time you will pay a penalty. So you will not normally be able to remortgage without paying a hefty fine, even if a much better deal comes along. With many lenders you will not be able to move home either. So you will be stuck where you are, whatever happens – including death, divorce, new job or quadruplet grandchildren – unless you bite the bullet and pay the fine. At the end of your deal, whether it is fixed, discounted, capped, or an exotic mixture of all three, your loan will continue at the lender's SVR. Lenders, of course, hope you will not notice and will carry on paying a much higher rate on your loan. And some lenders will still impose a penalty for a time after the good deal has come to an end.

Never, ever take on a mortgage deal where the penalty lasts longer than the deal. That will be very expensive when your deal comes to an end, but you have to carry on paying the SVR for a year or more. So the penalty or tie-in must not be longer than the deal.

Whatever mortgage you take out nowadays, you will have to pay a hefty fee just for becoming a customer. It is as if a supermarket charged you a fiver for walking into the shop. This fee has various names such as 'arrangement fee', 'booking fee' or 'administration fee' – all of which is rubbish. Its real purpose is to bring in more money, to help keep the mortgage rate low and tempt you into the deal.

These fees can be a fixed amount or even a percentage of the amount you borrow. That can make them very expensive indeed. Some lenders will offer you various combinations of fee and mortgage rate such as 6.64 per cent with a £649 fee or 6.04 per cent with a £1,995 fee. All these deals are designed to confuse, but they are now part of the mortgage world. It is impossible to see what is best without a computer and a lot of knowledge. That is why you employ a broker.

There will also be other costs to pay. Lawyers will want legal fees, valuers will be needed to make sure the property is worth as much as the loan, and of course your broker may charge you a fee, too. Some deals will come with 'free legals' or 'free valuation'. Again, this is confusion marketing designed to bamboozle you. Choosing between one interest rate and arrangement fee with free legals and another different rate and arrangement fee with free valuation is, literally, impossible. Get your broker to sort it out. And try to make sure the lender – who has caused all this confusion in the first place – pays him and you do not.

Yes, but remember I'm 50/60/70 Your age only matters if you don't – or won't – have the income to make the repayments. Normally a lender will assume you work until 65 if you are an employee or 70 if you are self-employed. So any mortgage deal will not stretch beyond that birthday unless you can show that other income from a pension or investments will be sufficient to meet the repayments. By the time you are 65 or 70 it is probably sensible to have paid off the mortgage anyway.

Changing your mortgage can easily save you £1,000 a year. But all those fees will probably eat up most of the saving or more for the first year or so. After that, you will be in the money. But when it ends you will have to do it all over again. ■

11
TAXING TIMES

TAXING TIMES

H M Revenue & Customs (HMRC, or 'the Revenue') admits that it takes too much tax off us – hundreds of millions of pounds each year. So it is up to all of us to make sure we do not pay too much. After all, it is our money. In the space available this guide cannot provide full information on paying less tax or checking how much you should pay. It will just deal with the basics, and especially where things often go wrong. And it just covers income tax – inheritance tax gets its own section (pages 210–16).

INCOME TAX BASICS

Income tax should be easy. Each year you can have a certain amount of income without any tax being due on it; income above that amount is taxed. What could be simpler? But for two centuries accountants, lawyers and, of course, politicians have earned a very good living out of making sure it is not as simple as that. So we have to get to grips with some of the complexities to begin to see if we are paying the right amount.

The tax year runs from 6 April to 5 April the following year, e.g. 6 April 2008 to 5 April 2009. In that year you can have an income of £5,435 before any tax is due. This is called your personal allowance. All that means is that you are 'allowed' to have that much income without paying any income tax on it. If you are at least 65 by the end of the tax year – hence, your 65th birthday is on 5 April 2009 or earlier – you can have a much higher income before tax is due: £9,030. If you are ten years older than that the allowance is £9,180. These are normally called 'age allowances'. If you are registered blind you can add £1,800 – called a 'blind person's allowance' – to any of these amounts.

All of these allowances go up each tax year. So they will be higher in 2009/10 and future tax years.

People under the age of 65 do not get the higher tax allowances, even if they have retired and get the state pension. A lot of women find that very unfair. It is. But it will slowly disappear as the pension age for women is raised to 65 by April 2020.

Income above your tax allowance is normally taxed at 20 per cent. This is called the basic rate. So if you have £1,000 more than the allowance you will pay £200 in tax. There are two exceptions to that rule. If you have a small amount of savings income above that limit it will be taxed at 10 per cent (that weird and complex rule is explained later). And if you have any dividends from shares then they will be paid to you with the tax already taken off. That rate is always 10 per cent. Once your income exceeds the tax allowance by about £36,000 the amount above that is taxed at 40 per cent. That is called higher-rate tax.

So far, so simple.

The allowance relates to the whole tax year. So in theory we could all be paid our pension, wages, savings interest and so on without any tax taken off and then settle up at the end of the year. But for everyone's convenience – not least the Revenue's – it doesn't work like that. That is where the mistakes creep in.

PAYE

Pay As You Earn (PAYE) is a sensible system which divides up your annual tax allowance into twelve monthly or 52 weekly amounts. Each month or week that amount is tax-free and the rest is taxed.

It has two advantages. First, you pay your tax as you go and never have to worry about it. Second, the Revenue gets its hands on the money earlier than it otherwise would. But the system has two huge disadvantages.

It only works well when you have one regular source of income which does not change much and your tax allowances do not change either. If any of those factors change during the tax year, PAYE finds it hard to cope. People on PAYE used to get a notice each year showing their tax code – a set of numbers and a letter which tells your employer or pension provider how much tax to deduct. Nowadays, the Revenue only sends these out if things change. If you do get one it will be called a P2 Notice of Coding and will explain how the tax has been worked out. You can find the explanation online at www.hmrc.gov.uk/p2

NOTICE OF CODING

The numbers in the code represent the amount of tax-free money you can have in the year. So if you have the standard allowance of £5,435 the code will be the first three of those digits: 543. After the number will be a letter:

L	Personal allowance under 65
P	Personal age-related allowance aged 65–74
V	Age-related allowance and full married couple's allowance, both under 75 and tax due at basic rate
Y	Personal allowance aged 75 or more
T	None of these codes describes your circumstances or you have asked the tax office to keep your tax code letter secret.

If you get a state pension your tax code is reduced. That is because your pension is taxable but is paid without any tax being deducted. So if your allowance is £5,435 and your pension is £90 a week or £4,680 a year that is deducted from the allowance to leave £755 and your tax code is 75L. Any income you have above £755 a year is taxed because your state pension has used up most of your tax-free allowance. It is very important to check that the amount deducted for your state retirement pension is accurate – it may not be.

Women who are under 65 do not get the age allowance. They can easily find that their state pension is more than their tax allowance. If that applies to you, you will get a special tax code (K) to collect the tax due on your pension. See box overleaf for example.

You can also have unpaid tax or interest which is paid gross put into your coding, so you pay a bit more tax on the rest of your income. These are all approximate ways of collecting the tax due. It is very

JOAN GETS A K CODE

Joan, 62, gets a full state pension of £90.70 a week plus some SERPS worth £24.30 a week on top. Altogether she gets £115 a week. That is £5,980 a year, which is £545 above her tax-free allowance. So Joan will get a rather strange code: it will start with the letter K followed by 54. The code K54 means she has to be taxed on an extra £540 of income (the £545 is rounded down). So she will end up paying slightly more than the basic rate of 20 per cent on all her earned income.

important to remember that tax codes are a way of collecting tax, *not* of assessing it. So you may end up paying too little or too much tax during the tax year. If that happens, you can get your tax adjusted after the end of the tax year.

Older married couples can get extra tax relief called 'married couple's allowance'. It is given to a married couple (or civil partners) only when at least one of them was born *before* 6 April 1935. Despite its name it is not an allowance but simply a deduction from your tax at the end of the tax year. The Revenue attempts to take account of it in your tax code but the adjustment may well give the wrong result. So it is highly recommended that anyone who gets the married couple's allowance, and has a tax code, should check that the correct tax has been deducted at the end of the year.

Because of all these complexities even the Revenue admits that it gets the tax wrong in lots of cases. It admits it collected £340 million too much through PAYE in 2006/7. Another £880 million was under-collected. Altogether up to 5 million taxpayers paid the wrong tax through PAYE. So it is very important to check your coding and at the end of the year check whether your tax is correct. Wait for your end-of-tax-year P60 from your employer or pension provider. That should show your income and how much tax you have paid in the tax year. Send a copy of that to your tax office explaining what you think is wrong.

TAX AND SAVINGS

The Revenue also likes to deduct tax automatically off any interest earned from savings or money in the bank. Your bank or building society automatically takes off 20 per cent from any interest earned and passes it to the Revenue. Do not blame them – this is the law. In many ways it is convenient for everyone.

However, each year millions of pounds are paid over that should not be. The Revenue once estimated that it had £300 million sitting in its coffers that should never have been deducted. It has even held several 'Taxback' campaigns and has a taxback helpline. But it still has huge amounts of tax that savers who do not pay tax could claim back but have not. And every year it collects more.

If you pay tax on earnings or a pension at the basic rate, you need not worry. The automatic deduction of tax from your interest will produce the right answer. But if your total income is less than your tax allowance you can tell the bank or building society to stop deducting the tax automatically. You do that on form R85, which the bank should have.

A couple in which one partner does not pay tax should consider transferring any savings to that person's name so that tax is no longer deducted. However, the gift of the money must be absolute, so if they later split up that could cause problems.

If you have had tax wrongly deducted from your savings interest you can claim it back. You can go back six whole tax years. You do that using another form, P40. You will need one for each tax year.

The forms can be downloaded from the Revenue's website, www.hmrc.gov.uk/taxback, which has a lot of useful information. You can register to receive interest gross by calling 0845 980 0645 and find out about claiming overpaid tax back from 0845 077 6543.

There is one further complexity about the tax on savings interest. Although it is deducted at 20 per cent it might – just might – only be due at 10 per cent. Imagine your income in two layers. At the bottom are your pension, wages and any income from rent. Floating on top of that – like the cream – is your savings interest. If the line which separates the two is less than the total of your personal allowance plus £2,320 the savings interest from that line up to the total will be taxed at just 10 per cent. The rest will be taxed at 20 per cent. But tax will still be deducted at the full rate of 20 per cent *on the whole lot* and it will be up to you to claim any excess back.

MAVIS CLAIMS TAX BACK

Mavis is 61 and has a small pension which she supplements with some part-time earnings. Her income from those two sources is £7,255. She also has about £12,000 in a good savings account which earns her £700 a year before tax is deducted. Her personal allowance is £5,435. She adds on £2,320 to give £7,755. Her other income is £500 below that. So the first £500 of her savings income will be taxed at 10 per cent and the remaining £200 at 20 per cent. The bank deducts the full 20 per cent from all of it, which is £140. She can claim back £50, the extra tax charged on the first £500.

Fiddly, or what? Anyone would think the Revenue did not want people to work it out and claim it back ...

The figure of £2,320 is an estimate for 2008/9 and will change each year along with the personal allowances. The system – which only began in 2008/9 – is so complicated it may not last for many more years.

SELF-ASSESSMENT

Two words that strike fear into 10 million people each year are 'self-assessment'. Once the form arrives it takes on its own momentum. You have to fill it in, by a certain date – or face a fine. This quick tour round the tax system can only stop off briefly at self-assessment. Lots of people who get the form have limited incomes. But for them filling the form in, though daunting at first, should be relatively simple.

The important point about self-assessment is the deadline. The paper form has to be in by 31 October after you get it. If you make that deadline those kind people at the Revenue will tell you what tax you owe in time for you to send them a cheque by the payment deadline of 31 January. If you miss the 31 October deadline you can file online right up to 31 January. If you miss that second filing deadline you are fined. The penalty is £100 but if you owe less than that in tax the penalty is no more than the tax you owe. So if in fact you owe nothing there is no penalty. If you pay the tax due after 31 January the Revenue will charge you interest and other penalties, which will increase with time.

You can get advice on self-assessment, including in the evening and at weekends, by calling the HM Revenue & Customs Self-assessment Helpline on 0845 9000 444.

TAX ON HIGHER INCOMES

The higher tax allowances for people aged 65 or more get a bit complicated when your income exceeds a certain amount. If it is more than £21,800 (in 2008/9 – like everything that will change each year) your age allowance is reduced. For every £2 of extra income above £21,800 your allowance will be reduced by £1.

For example, if you are 65 and your total income in 2008/9 is £23,800 your allowance will be reduced by £2,000 ÷ 2 = £1,000. That will take it down from £9,030 to £8,030. The allowance is never reduced below the basic personal allowance of £5,435 which happens when your income reaches £28,990 or more (aged 65–74) or £29,290 or more (aged 75 or over) in 2008/9.

When you are working out your income to see what personal allowance you will get, you have to use a particular figure called 'total gross income'. All income has to be 'gross', which means before any tax is deducted. So add up your pension or wages before the tax has been taken off through PAYE. Any savings income which has had tax already deducted must have that tax added back. You do that by dividing the interest by 4 and multiplying by 5. If you get dividends on shares, you must also add on the gross dividend to work out whether you are entitled to the higher allowance.

Then you have to take off any payments to charity made under Gift Aid. Again, gross them up by dividing the amount you gave by 4 and multiplying by 5. So if you paid £50 under Gift Aid, you divide by 4 and multiply by 5, which gives £62.50 and you can deduct that from your income. You can also deduct any payments you make yourself into a pension scheme.

The final figure is your 'total gross income' and it is that amount which determines whether your age allowance will be reduced and by how much.

You can find out more about tax from the free Help the Aged leaflet *Check Your Tax*, which is published each year and contains all the latest tax allowances and information. If you have a low income you can get help with any tax questions from two organisations that use professional tax advisers. They are

- TaxAid 0845 120 3779 (10am–noon, Mondays–Thursdays) www.taxaid.org.uk
- Tax Help for Older People 0845 601 3321 www.taxvol.org.uk

There is also a special section for older people on the Low Incomes Tax Reform website at www.litrg.org.uk

PART III

LIFE EVENTS

Parts I and II of the guide help you boost income or cut expenditure. But the best-laid schemes of mice and men (and women) and all that ... So Part III is about life shocks that can send anyone off course. It is also about big changes that are, if not inevitable, then at least pretty likely – such as dying. All these things get rather more likely, or at least closer, as we head for and into retirement. Planning for them can make them less of a problem for you and your heirs.

12
SUDDEN SHOCKS

When bad things such as redundancy, divorce, or a serious accident or illness hit us in mid-life, they can have a greater effect than when we were younger and had more time in which to get over the impact. This section looks at some of these crises and how the financial blow – at least – can be reduced.

REDUNDANCY

Redundancy is a great fear for people in their 50s. Just when you expect to have a clear view of the horizon of retirement, you suddenly find you are there, over the edge, just when you least expect it – and often cannot really afford it.

The first thing to consider is whether the redundancy is voluntary or compulsory. The difference can be quite subtle and it is actually better if even a voluntary redundancy is treated as a compulsory one.

Redundancy is a valid reason for dismissing someone but it has to be done correctly. Technically it means that the company no longer needs that particular job to be filled. Perhaps the advance of technology means it is simply not needed. Perhaps there has been a reduction in that business activity. Or maybe the company has to save money and other people will just have to cope by filling the gap left. Efficiency often means fewer people doing the same amount of work. It is important to realise that it is the post, not the person, that is made redundant. So once the employee has gone the business cannot just fill the job again with a new job-holder. This applies equally to compulsory or voluntary redundancy.

Redundancy is a dismissal. If you volunteer for redundancy it is important to make sure that your employer does actually dismiss you and sends you a letter setting out the terms of your dismissal and confirming that it is due to redundancy. Without that, you may find problems when you come to claim benefits or if you want to claim on an insurance policy that protects your income.

If you are made redundant against your wishes it is very important that the employer has made the selection for redundancy fairly. If you do not want to be made redundant and you suspect that your post has been chosen because it is you, you may have a case for unfair dismissal.

Think, for example, about the following:

- were you a member of the trade union or particularly active in it?
- do you have childcare or other caring responsibilities?
- were you pregnant?
- do you have an illness or disability?
- did you insist on your right to work the proper hours under the Working Time Directive?
- have you been a whistleblower?
- did you demand the national minimum wage?
- are you over 50?

If so, you may have a case for unfair dismissal. To find out what steps to take, contact your union, ACAS or the Tribunals Service (see chapter 14), or seek help at a local Citizens Advice office.

People, especially older ones, working in the public sector or in one of the diminishing number of companies with a decent pension scheme are often targeted with promises of pension protection, large redundancy payments and sessions with redundancy counsellors. Employers know that people are attracted by the idea of being able to take away a large lump sum and a pension, and that they do not necessarily think through how they will live in five years' time.

Employers may prefer to make older employees redundant because it frees up the promotion ladder for younger people, which is supposed to boost morale lower down; and managers want new blood and assume that people who have been doing a job for some years are stale. Both these reasons are ageist – they discriminate solely on grounds of age – and many companies which have followed them to get rid of many people over 45 realise too late that they have lost the collective memory of the company. Nowadays, to remove people from their jobs on grounds of age is unlawful.

There is also a very practical reason why companies try to bias redundancy towards older workers. Many salary structures used to give increments for length of service. So if there are two people doing the same job, the one with long service in the company will be paid more, sometimes a lot more, than the other. So getting rid of long-serving staff, who by their nature will tend to be older, saves more money, both on salary and pension contributions, than making newer employees redundant. That is why enhanced terms are often offered – it costs the company money this year but saves it money in future years. Sometimes these deals will be offered with very little time to decide. Treat that like any offer you are pressured into taking – ask for more time and do not accept it if this is refused.

REDUNDANCY PAY

If you have been working for your employer for at least two years you will normally be entitled to statutory redundancy pay. It does not matter whether you worked full- or part-time. The minimum amount of redundancy pay is determined by how long you have worked for that employer and your age. You are entitled to one week's pay for each year's service aged 22–40 and 1½ weeks' pay for each year you worked from the age of 41. There is no upper age limit any more – you can get redundancy pay whatever age you are if you are dismissed due to redundancy.

The maximum number of years of service that can count is 20 and so the maximum entitlement is 30 weeks' pay. There is also an upper limit – and quite a low one – on a week's pay. In 2008 it is £330. So the total statutory redundancy pay cannot be more than £9,900. If your employer has gone bust, the Department of Trade and Industry will pay the money to you. You can get help and advice from the Insolvency Service Redundancy Payments Office on 0845 145 00 04. It will help with your rights and tell you which local Redundancy Payments Office you should be in touch with. If your former employer is not bust but refuses to pay your redundancy money, you may have to go to an employment tribunal. Get help from your union or from Citizens Advice.

Many people are entitled to more than the statutory minimum. Your contract of employment may specify, for example, a month's pay for each year's service. If you are taking voluntary redundancy, the company may be prepared to pay even more as part of a package deal. Redundancy payments are tax-free up to a maximum of £30,000, but do make sure that you are made redundant properly and lawfully otherwise HMRC may challenge the tax-free status of the payment and say it was in fact early retirement or that you just left of your own accord. If it does, you should appeal, as mistakes – usually to the benefit of HMRC – are common. If you get paid more than £30,000, the excess is taxable as income in the tax year it is received.

When you leave you will also get all the wages that are owed to you, including any amounts owing for holiday pay or pay in lieu of notice. All those amounts will be taxed before you receive them. Any payment you are entitled to under your contract of employment just because you leave the company – sometimes called severance pay – is also taxable as income and tax will be deducted before you receive it. One way round this rule is to get any taxable money paid into your pension instead. You can then take a quarter of it out tax-free and the rest will boost your pension. If you get an extra payment out of the goodness of the employer's heart – usually called an ex *gratia** payment – that will not be taxable. But it can be very hard to prove that it was ex *gratia*. It must be nothing to do with your accepting the redundancy and not a payment you are entitled to in your contract.

*Latin moment: ex *gratia*, which literally translates as 'by favour', means that the giver receives nothing at all from it – except perhaps a warm glow.

NEXT STEPS AFTER REDUNDANCY

Losing your job in mid- or later life is frightening, even if you have volunteered for it. If you hear you are going to be made redundant, take time to recover from the shock before you make any plans. Your redundancy pay may seem like a lot of tax-free cash, but it will soon disappear. So treat your new-found freedom as a time to look for new work rather than as a long holiday with pay, bearing in mind that there may be no work – and little income – when the redundancy money runs out.

DIVORCE

A growing number of couples over 50 are deciding to end their marriages – often very long-term ones. Although the total number of divorces fell by more than 9 per cent between 1991 and 2001, among people aged 45 and more the numbers rose. That is especially true for people in their 50s: divorce was up by 40 per cent for men and by 50 per cent for women over that ten-year period. The rate is still rising. In 2004 – the latest detailed statistics available – more than 25,000 men and 19,000 women in their 50s got divorced. Nearly 13,000 people divorcing that year were in their 60s. Finding yourself alone at any age is hard, but the older you are the more difficult it can be. The only positive is that children – or at least young children – are less likely to be involved.

Most people who divorce over 50 want what is called a 'clean break' – in other words, they split their jointly owned property and go their separate ways with neither depending on the other financially in the future. It may not always seem very fair, but generally the courts will try to ensure that a wife and husband divide all their assets equally, regardless of who brought what to the marriage or who contributed most financially during it. Pre-nuptial agreements, which set out who owns what before the marriage and try to protect assets belonging to one partner, generally do not work in the UK. Although the courts will consider them, judges have the power to decide what is fair regardless of what any agreement says.

Your assets do not just include your possessions and your home.

They include money, savings, investments and nowadays the pension rights of each partner. Splitting savings, investments, valuables and movable property like furniture is normally quite straightforward. But do remember that dividing a set of six chairs into three each means they are worth a lot less to both of you than a set of six is to one partner.

The assets that are hardest to deal with are your home and your pension rights – though of course if you jointly own a business that can get very messy and you will need legal advice. You will also find how true is the old saying that two can live as cheaply as one. A separated couple will need two washing machines, two televisions, two computers, perhaps two cars, and, of course, two places to live. Try to ensure that you share out the difficulties and that you both live slightly worse off rather than one partner carrying on as before and the other putting up with all the privations.

WHAT HAPPENS TO THE MARITAL HOME

If you divorce, your home may have to be sold. Anyone in their 50s who is left without a home may have problems buying a replacement. First, they may have only a small share of the value of the original home to put against a new one. Second, if they have to arrange a mortgage, lenders will assume they will stop working at 65 – or 70 if self-employed. That means that a repayment mortgage will be an expensive option with far less time than is normal to repay the loan. If you are in that position you could consider an interest-only mortgage, relying perhaps on a pension lump sum, an inheritance or good fortune to repay the capital. You need to be confident and a good sleeper to be able to do that.

Lenders will also want to be sure that you have the income to meet the repayments. Normally maintenance payments from your ex-husband or wife will not be counted as income – unless they are secured by a court order and you are borrowing less than 75 per cent of the value of the property. It is also difficult for one partner to get a mortgage on a new property if they still have a mortgage remaining on the first. You need a good mortgage broker to sort these problems out. If you remarry, remember that any will you have made prior to that remarriage will be invalid. Also remember that a new spouse will immediately acquire rights to your property, including property your children may at some stage expect to inherit. If you die and your new spouse marries again, the property could end up a long way from your original family.

DIVORCE AND PENSIONS

The right to a pension is a very valuable asset. In a marriage it is normally assumed that the pension will provide, at least partly, for both partners. But it is only fairly recently that its value has formed a separate part of the assets which can be shared between the partners on divorce. There are three ways in which a pension can be shared. The first step is to get the pension fund or insurance company to provide the court with what is called a cash equivalent transfer value (CETV). The value of each partner's pension is then counted as an asset. Remember that public sector jobs (including teachers, nurses, and civil servants) bring with them valuable salary-related pensions. A woman who earns much less than her husband may find the value of her public sector pension is more than the value of his money-purchase or personal pension that has no guarantees with it.

Once the value has been obtained, it can be split three ways.

1 Its value can simply be counted as part of the assets. One party may keep the whole of the pension as long as the other gets assets of an equivalent value. For example, if the CETV of the pension was £200,000 and the marital home was also valued at £200,000, one partner could have the house and the other the pension. This method is called 'offsetting' and is still the most common way of dealing with the problem, partly because it can be the most straightforward.

2 It can be 'earmarked', which means that when the person with the pension rights reaches the scheme's pension age, the scheme pays a pension not just to them but also to their ex-spouse. Earmarking began in 1996 but its limitations were soon realised and it is seldom used.

3 It can be split. Once the CETV has been obtained, if no other division of the assets would produce a fair settlement the pension itself can be split. For example, if a husband had an occupational pension which provided him with a pension of £25,000 a year, index-linked, as well as a widows' pension and a lump sum, a value would be put on this (probably about £500,000) and the pension fund would have to transfer half of that sum to a pension in his ex-wife's name. She would have to use it to buy a pension herself from a pension provider.

These deals can be very complex and the ideal, of course, is for both parties to come to an amicable agreement – with the help of their solicitors – and leave the courts out of it. Pension-splitting and the CETV do help achieve a result that is genuinely fair to both partners, but it is still very rare and many solicitors are not very good at the complex calculations involved. You can find lawyers who specialise in amicable and efficient divorces through Resolution, which has more than 5,000 registered solicitors. See www.resolution.org.uk or call 01689 820272.

The SERPS or S2P part of a state pension (see pages 46–7) is treated like a pension from a job or a personal pension and can be split or shared in the same way. The basic state pension is treated differently. Once you are divorced, each partner can use the other's National Insurance contributions instead of their own, either for their whole working life or for the time they were married. Usually this means that a woman who has an inadequate National Insurance contribution record can get a full record and a full pension. So make sure that HMRC and the Department for Work and Pensions knows about your divorce so that your state pension entitlement is worked out correctly. Using your ex-spouse's contributions does not affect their state pension at all.

If you remarry before state pension age, you lose the right to use your former spouse's contribution record. However, once you have reached pension age and claimed your state pension – using your ex-spouse's contributions if possible – the pension is not taken away if you marry. So if you are divorced it may be worth considering putting off remarriage until you have reached pension age and claimed your pension.

SEPARATION

If you separate rather than divorce you are still married as far as the law is concerned. So for most financial arrangements separation has no effect. The one exception is entitlement to means-tested benefits such as Income Support, Council Tax Benefit, Pension Credit and tax credits. They are calculated on joint income for couples who live together, whether married, civil partners or neither.

Separated people who live alone have their own income counted separately. An occupational pension will still be paid to the person who has earned it. The separated partner will still have rights to a pension as a widow or widower when their separated partner dies. You will still be treated as married when your basic state pension is worked out. So if you are a married woman with no rights to a pension yourself, you will just get the married woman's pension instead of the full pension. Hence, if you are separated, you may want to consider divorce — it can boost your income and it may give you other rights to half your spouse's property.

All those comments and rules apply of course equally to same-sex couples who have entered into a civil partnership which, although it is not called marriage, is just about identical.

UNMARRIED COUPLES

Couples who are not married are in a much more difficult position.

Marriage is less popular than it has ever been. Fewer than 250,000 people marry each year: half the number who wed a generation ago. Today there are 2 million people in unmarried couples and more than three-quarters of a million of them are over 45. Many younger couples live together as a prelude to marriage, but older couples tend to remain unmarried.

Outside Scotland, couples who live together in the UK without being married generally have no rights at all over each other's property. Women in particular should be aware that living together confers no financial rights whatsoever. You can live with someone for years, decorate their home, cook their meals and have their children without gaining a single financial right to their property – including the home you share – if it is 'his' rather than 'yours'. That can come as a major shock when the relationship breaks down. Marriage gives much more security for the financially weaker partner. That is worth remembering that when a new relationship is formed, especially by the person who earns the least and has the least in terms of property or possessions – which is normally the woman.

In Scotland unmarried partners now have some rights over some of each other's property if they can show that the relationship breakdown has caused them some 'economic disadvantage' compared with the other partner. There are proposals to introduce something similar in England and Wales, but these laws are much weaker than the rights which married couples and civil partners have.

Even determined cohabitants may want to consider marriage later in life. It can make things much simpler for the partner who survives. For more on the reasons for that see the section on inheritance tax, pages 210–16.

ILLNESS AND DISABILITY

One of the less pleasant aspects of reaching your 50s is a sense that your body is not as strong or supple as it once was and you have less energy. It can creep up on you slowly, but perhaps when you dash for a bus, play with your grandchild or have to decorate the kitchen you realise you are getting older. Of course, these changes happen at different times and different rates. But they happen to us all. Sadly, what started as an ache or shortage of breath can turn from ageing into disability. It can be hard to admit that the old ankle injury or the back pain you have lived with for years has now become a disability, but it is important that you do.

Information about benefits and help from the state is in chapter 3. But if you are still at work, you may want to talk to your employer about early retirement on health grounds. Certainly you should let them know of any impairment you are living with. Many employers will be helpful and sympathetic, not least because having a person who is technically disabled can help them reach quotas and show they do not discriminate. Remember, it is now illegal to discriminate against anyone on those grounds. For example, you cannot be dismissed or made redundant just because of a disability.

Just as disability creeps upon us as we get older, so does caring. As we reach our 50s, the older generation reaches its 80s and 90s and becomes dependent on others for its care and happiness. It is often a matter of luck who ends up with that responsibility. For more about carers and Carer's Allowance see pages 55–6.

Your local council can help you with information and practical services. As a carer you have a right to an assessment by the social services department of your local council. The assessment will focus on what you need as a carer, although whether the social services department will have the money or ability to provide the services or help you need is another matter. If you are working and caring, you do have limited rights to 'reasonable' time off to help people who are dependent on you. You can get more information about assessments for carers and carers' rights from Carers UK (see chapter 14). Carers UK will also be able to tell you whether there is a carers' support group locally. ■

13
LOOKING AHEAD

M id-life is a time to face the fact that we are not immortal. The life ahead is not infinite, and one of the best things we can do for our nearest and dearest is to leave a valid will and perhaps do some other planning that will help them after we are gone.

Now is also the time to think about how well we will be able to cope as we get older, and the possibility that we might one day need care and support to a greater or lesser degree.

WILLS

One well-known accountant, a frequent contributor to BBC programmes, says that we should all have a 'dying tidily' file where we set down what we own, what we pay out, details of our bank accounts and investments and of any pension or income we have. Central to the file should, of course, be a will.

Everyone knows they should have a will, but at least half the adult population does not. Of course, until you die it does not matter and many people put it off until later in life. But once you are in your 50s death is undoubtedly closer and it is a mistake to delay any longer. Also, bear in mind that there are huge disadvantages to dying without a will.

First, your property may not go to the person you want it to go to. Dying without a will – 'intestate' – means that your possessions are divided up according to strict legal rules under which husbands or wives may not get everything. Children also have a claim, as do brothers and sisters. Even a distant cousin may end up with some of it. If no relatives can be found, the whole estate will go to the Treasury. What could be worse than that?

Second, having no will makes life very difficult for the people who survive you who have to sort out your affairs. It is much easier for them if they have your own wishes to follow in a will rather than having to grapple with the laws of intestacy.

You can draw up a will yourself if your circumstances are very simple and straightforward: kits are available in newsagents and on the internet. But it is much more sensible to get it drawn up by a professional. That way you can be sure it does what you want.

So do not look on making a will as morbid. It is not. It is a loving act for those you will leave behind.

A free leaflet entitled *Making a Will* can be downloaded from the Help the Aged website, www.helptheaged.org.uk.

INHERITANCE TAX

People get very worked up about inheritance tax (IHT). But the truth is that most people do not have enough money or property for any IHT to be due on their estate at all.

It is due if you die and leave more than £312,000 in 2008/9; that amount will rise to £325,000 for deaths occurring in 2009/10 and £350,000 in 2010/11. Even counting the value of their home most people have far less than that. New rules introduced in October 2007 mean that widowed men and women can usually leave twice that much without any tax being due. Those rules are a bit complex (what a surprise) and are explained on pages 211–12.

People fear the tax because they see the value of their home rising and rising and they expect that by the time they die that could be enough in itself to exceed the limit. But the Government has committed itself to raising the threshold for the tax in future, taking account of house prices as well as inflation. So the chances are that if you are not liable now you will not be liable in future. So why not find out if your heirs would have to pay inheritance tax if you were to die now?

Step 1 Add up the value of your house, your savings, any investments, valuables you own including jewellery, and any other personal possessions that have a value. You must include money or property that you own anywhere in the world.

Step 2 If you have given away money or property worth more than about £3,000 in any of the last seven years, add that on too. Do not add on anything you have given away more than seven years ago.

Step 3 Take away any debts you have – including a mortgage, a credit card, an overdraft, or a loan. If you have taken out an equity release plan on your home, deduct the full value of that. When you die, any unpaid bills and the costs of your funeral will be deducted from your estate.

Step 4 Deduct anything you intend to leave to your spouse or civil partner. Everything you leave to them is free of inheritance tax without limit as long as you both normally live in the UK.

Step 5 Deduct anything you intend to leave to charity.

After adding up steps 1 and 2 and deducting steps 3, 4, and 5, is the answer £312,000 or less? If it is, no tax will be due if you die in 2008/9. If you are a widow or widower the threshold will usually be twice that amount: £624,000 in 2008/9. So in most cases no tax will be due. If the Government keeps to its word and takes account of house prices when it fixes the IHT threshold, this should mean that if your estate is below the limit today it will be below it when you do eventually die.

If the amount is more than the threshold IHT is charged at 40 per cent of the surplus above the threshold. So on an estate worth £412,000 the tax is 40 per cent of £100,000 – which is £40,000. But on a widow's estate no tax would be due at that level. Her estate would have to be £724,000 before tax was due on £100,000.

This is how those widow's rules work.

The new rules allow a higher threshold when a widow dies. That includes widowers and bereaved civil partners but for simplicity let us call all of them widows. Their heirs count one allowance for the newly deceased widow and can also add on the unused allowance of the widow's late spouse. That means many widows or widowers who die will have a double inheritance tax allowance. In 2008/9 that means no tax will be due if their estate is up to £624,000 instead of the £312,000 allowed to single people.

If the first spouse to die leaves everything to the surviving spouse, when the latter dies the allowance is doubled.

If the first spouse to die has left money or property to other people, some allowance can still be passed on. The amount they left to people other than their spouse is worked out as a proportion of the allowance that was current at the time. For example, if the first spouse died in 2002/3 when the allowance was £250,000 and they left £50,000 directly to their children, they have used up 50 ÷ 250 or 20 per cent of their allowance. That leaves 80 per cent to be passed on to the survivor.

When the surviving spouse dies they get their own allowance plus the unused percentage multiplied by the current allowance. So if the second spouse dies in 2009/10 when the allowance is £325,000 her heirs will get:

- her own allowance of £325,000 and
- £325,000 × 80% = £260,000 as her inherited allowance

– making a total of £585,000. No tax will be due if she leaves less than that. Inheritance Tax will be due on anything she leaves above £585,000.

Of course, if the first to die leaves property or money to other people which uses up the whole of their allowance there will be no allowance to pass on to the survivor.

The new rules on inheritance tax apply only to people who were married or civil partners at the time of the first death. If they simply lived together or had divorced before the first died, no allowance can be passed on. However, a widow who remarries and is bereaved again can inherit an allowance from both late spouses. But the total inherited allowance cannot be more than 100 per cent.

There is no time limit to the date of widowhood so even someone who was widowed 40 years ago may still have an inherited allowance to pass on. The Revenue has produced a complete list of thresholds right back to 1914 at www.hmrc.gov.uk/cto/customerguide/page15.htm

The new rules mean that the safest advice for married couples is to leave everything to their spouse. If you want property or valuables to go to your heirs, tell your spouse and trust the survivor to make those gifts later. When the second spouse dies the heirs will benefit from the double IHT threshold.

In the past the rules were different and some couples will already have written wills to leave some of their property to children or other heirs. Some couples arranged to leave half their home to their children. That is usually not necessary now. Remember that a will can be rewritten for up to two years after a death as long as all the heirs agree.

However, in one circumstance it may still be better to consider splitting the value of the property. If a widow or widower remarries and already has 100 per cent of their late spouse's allowance to inherit it may be worth splitting the estate so that each leaves half to their heirs. If you are in this position, seek advice.

IHT AND UNMARRIED COUPLES

Couples who are not married do not have the advantages of married couples and civil partners. No IHT exemption is available on gifts or inheritance between you. So if your home is worth more than the IHT threshold and the one who owns the house dies and leaves the property to their partner, the survivor can face a big IHT bill just to remain in the home. That can happen even if you own half the property if it is worth more than twice the IHT threshold. If you are determined not to marry – or for legal reasons cannot – there is little you can do about this danger, but you should be aware of it. The only concession is that the Revenue will let you pay the tax due on a property in ten annual instalments, but interest will be charged on the amount due.

In Scotland a new status of 'cohabitant' has been created, but although this gives unmarried couples some rights to each other's property on separation or death it does not change the rules to allow them to inherit from each other without paying tax. There are plans for a similar change in England and Wales, but that will not address the problems of inheritance tax either.

If you are free to marry there is nothing to stop you indulging – if that is the word – in a deathbed marriage. That can help your heirs as well now that married couples can pass on their own unused allowance to the heirs when the second dies. This is something to think about if one of you has an illness which seems to point to an early death, or if you have been living together for years and are now in your 50s.

REDUCING IHT

The best way to reduce the IHT that has to be paid is to spend your money now to make sure your estate is worth less than the threshold.

Gifts made more than seven years before your death are not counted at all when IHT is worked out. So the best option is to give money away and live another seven years. Other gifts are not counted even if you do die within seven years of making them.

You can of course give any amount away to your husband, wife or civil partner. You can also make any number of small gifts of up to £250 each to any number of people. So if you transfer £100 to your grandchildren on their birthdays and Christmas that does not count at all.

One little-known exemption is that you can make a regular gift of money out of income that you do not need. That might happen, for example, if a widow inherited a pension from her husband but found she could not really spend it all now she was by herself. If her bank balance keeps growing each month she can give that surplus away regularly – perhaps, say, helping to support a young relative at college.

A wedding allows you to make more generous gifts without them counting. If it is your own child you can give up to £5,000. A grandchild (or great-grandchild) can be given up to £2,500 and anyone you wish can have up to £1,000.

If your child is in full-time education you can give them money to maintain them and pay their education costs. So you can pay university tuition fees and give money for living expenses. But the student must be your child – not a grandchild.

You can also give any amount to a major political party, a registered charity, a national museum or art gallery, or a university.

Finally, you can give away other gifts up to a total of £3,000 in a year. You can also carry this allowance forward from the previous year, so that it can be worth £6,000 if you gave nothing the previous year.

All these exemptions are individual – so a husband and wife can give these amounts each. Hence, a couple who have not really thought about reducing IHT can give away £12,000 between them in one tax year without it counting for IHT at all. Even if one spouse owns the money they can give £6,000 to their spouse and then each can give £6,000 to, say, their child.

However, although giving away money can help reduce IHT, you should never give away money that you will need yourself. Your heirs will not thank you if you give them generous gifts and then a few years later ask for help – probably long after they have spent the money.

When people first come across inheritance tax they always try to think of simple ways to avoid it. One of the most popular ideas is to give away something but still keep using it. For example, people often have the bright idea that they can give away their home to their children but carry on living in it. So when they die, they believe, the house will not be theirs and will not count as part of their estate. Unfortunately that wheeze has been thought of. If you give away your home and continue to live in it, it will still count as part of your estate even if the legal title actually belongs to your children. The same is true if, for example, you give your daughter a valuable painting but keep it hanging on your walls.

If you have a life insurance policy the amount paid out to your heirs on your death can count as part of your estate and that can mean IHT is due on the payout. Avoiding that is very simple. Instead of paying out directly to your heirs the policy should be what is called 'written in trust'. This means that the money is paid into a trust, which passes it on to your dependants: this avoids the proceeds counting as part of your estate. However, if it is a large life insurance policy worth more than £312,000 some tax may be due from time to time. So you should consult your insurance company before taking this step.

If you are in business or farming there may well be other amounts you can deduct from your estate before IHT is calculated, so make sure your executors are aware of that.

LEAVING MONEY TO CHARITY

Sometimes people are advised to leave money to a charity as a way of reducing IHT. It is true that any money you leave to a charity does not count towards your estate when IHT is worked out. But that does not make it a sensible way to avoid paying inheritance tax.

For example, Stan dies in 2009/10 with an estate of £375,000. He decides to leave £50,000 to a cancer charity as his wife Beth had died of that disease. So his estate is £325,000 and no IHT is due as that is the threshold in 2009/10. His five children get £65,000 each. But if Stan had not made his generous gift they would have shared the whole estate. That was £375,000, which was £50,000 above the threshold, so tax of £20,000 was due – leaving £355,000 to share between them or £71,000 each. So they are left worse off. In general, heirs get more if you make no gifts to charity in your will. Now of course it is Stan's money and giving a substantial gift to the charity is a good thing. Many charities depend on legacy income to be able to carry out much of their work. But bear in mind that leaving money to a charity is not tax-planning.

IHT REDUCTION SCHEMES

Some financial advisers sell plans which they claim can reduce inheritance tax. These schemes are always complicated and usually involve making gifts into or from trusts. They often involve taking out an insurance policy – not least, of course, because insurance policies usually pay good commission and the main purpose of these schemes is often to generate rewards for the salesperson rather than actually benefit the client. Also, remember that by the time your heirs find it does not work as expected you will be dead and the salesperson will probably be long gone.

The Government has taken action to stop some of these schemes, and it has warned that it will take action against any scheme that achieves nothing but the reduction of tax. Trusts can be a way to avoid IHT but they can be expensive to set up and run, and are mainly suitable for people with estates worth considerably more than the IHT threshold. New restrictions mean they are less useful than they were in the past and the Government may restrict their use again.

For more information go to the HM Revenue & Customs website, www.hmrc.gov.uk/cto/iht.htm. Or you can call the Inheritance Tax & Probate helpline on 0845 302 0900.

CARE COSTS

Second only to inheritance tax are worries about paying for the cost of going into a care home. So here is a word of comfort at the start. Most people – about four out of five – never go into care, and most of those that do never pay a penny for it. However, that does not stop people worrying about it.

The reason is that they fear that they will have to sell their home to pay for their care. Now here is the really good news – no one ever has to sell their home to pay for their care. Anyone who tells you that you might either does not understand the rules or is deliberately telling you fibs to try to get money off you. Even if you did have to sell your home to pay for care, does it really matter? After all, the value of your home belongs to you. So why should it not be used to give you some care and comfort in your old age? Pause for thought.

RULES GOVERNING PAYMENT FOR CARE

If 'rules' had a plural such as 'ruleses' that would be appropriate because there are rules in England, different rules in Scotland, other rules in Wales, and yet a fourth set of rules in Northern Ireland (all thanks to devolution). However, the principle remains the same. You do not have to sell your home to pay for your care. One more time: *you do not have to sell your home to pay for your care.* That is because, one way or another, the NHS or the local council will usually pay for your care. If neither of them does, you still do not have to sell your home.

The big change in England at least is that the NHS will pay for care in far more circumstances than it used to. Anyone in a care home who needs continuing health care should have all the care home fees paid in full by the NHS. So the first thing to do if someone has to go into a care home is see if the NHS will pay. If the answer is 'no', appeal.

People who do not get all their costs paid by the NHS will have their care provided by the local council – in England, by the social services department. Although the local council provides the care it can charge the resident. To do that it applies a means test. Some people will get the bulk of the fees paid by the council, though most will have to pay something from their income or capital towards the cost. Others who have a high income or capital will have to pay the whole cost of their care.

Some of the residents who are not ill enough to be paid for in full by the NHS will nevertheless require some care from a registered nurse. If that is so, the NHS pays a flat weekly rate towards their nursing costs. The amount varies in the four countries (see table on page 220) and is not means-tested. If the resident pays in full for their own care they will get this NHS contribution as a reduction in the cost of their fees. If they do not pay their fees in full, the contribution will reduce the amount the local council pays towards their fees.

It is this means test that leads people to think that they will have to sell their home to pay for their care. If your capital is more than a certain amount – just over £20,000, but the amounts differ slightly across the four countries of the UK – no contribution to the fees is paid by the local council. Instead, you are expected to pay the fees out of the capital until it falls below that level. With fees up to and even over £750 a week, that may not take very long. When your capital is counted the value of your home can form part of it but is normally ignored. The value of the resident's home does not count as part of their capital:

- if their spouse or partner (including an unmarried partner) continues to live in it, or
- if another relative lives there as their home who is either aged 60+ or disabled.

So for many people the value of their home does not count at all. Even if no one lives there the value is ignored for the first 12 weeks in the care home. Only after that time can its value be counted as part of the resident's capital. That will normally mean that the resident has to pay the whole cost of their care themselves. But that does not mean the home has to be sold.

Instead, the Social Services Department will make a 'deferred payment agreement'. It continues to provide the care and the cost of the fees accumulates as a debt. Only when the resident eventually dies will the home have to be sold and the debt paid. This has three big advantages:

- even though the debt builds up, no interest is charged on it for the whole time the resident is alive and for 56 days after their death
- it may be possible to rent out the home to help pay for the cost of the care
- the value of the home will probably rise while the owner is in the care home.

As a result there will probably still be money left for the heirs when the resident eventually does die.

There are two other things to be aware of. Capital of about £13,000 is ignored completely along with any income it earns. Between that level and the upper limit a contribution of between £1 and £34 a week has to be made from the capital.

People who pay all their own fees may be able to claim a benefit called Attendance Allowance, which is worth up to £67 a week. Almost everyone ill enough to be in a home will be entitled to it. It can be claimed even if a contribution towards the nursing care is being paid by the NHS (though that is not true in Scotland). It can also be claimed even if the resident has made a deferred payment agreement on their home. Staff at the Department for Work and Pensions sometimes misunderstand these complex rules and wrongly refuse claims for Attendance Allowance to people in care homes who are in these two groups. If that happens the resident can ask for the decision to be revised or, if that does not work, go to appeal. Citizens Advice can help with appeals.

If you want to appeal it is sensible to get help from Citizens Advice or a welfare rights agency, or from SeniorLine, the Help the Aged telephone service (see chapter 14).

ENGLAND, SCOTLAND, WALES, NORTHERN IRELAND

All four countries have different rules about paying for care.

2007/8	England	Northern Ireland	Scotland	Wales
Capital ignored up to	£13,000	£13,000	£12,500	£17,250
Weekly contribution from capital	£1–£34	£1–£34	£1–£33	£1–£19
Upper capital limit for help with fees	£21,500	£21,500	£20,750	£22,000
Weekly nursing care contribution	£101	£100	£65*+145 towards social care (£210 total)	£114.90

* People who get the nursing contribution in Scotland lose entitlement to Attendance Allowance

MOVING ABROAD

As we get older many of us dream of giving it all up and moving abroad. And our 50s can seem just the right time to turn those dreams into reality. But there is a lot to consider before you sell up and commit yourself to living abroad for the rest of your life. It is a big risk and can be financially devastating.

People want to live abroad for many reasons. A warmer climate can mean better health. Cheaper property can mean a nicer home or spare cash to boost retirement income. Better – and cheaper – food and drink, as well as lower prices for clothes and other goods and services, mean a better standard of living. Sports and leisure activities can be more fun in the sun. Sometimes it is as simple as being able to have a nice breakfast on a sunny terrace every morning. Some of these dreams are illusions – what can seem great for a few weeks on holiday can disappoint rapidly if it is the whole of your life. On the other hand, rainy and expensive Britain, where every day seems to bring a new story of violence or disaster, can seem a miserable place to pass the last stages of your life.

On the other hand, you will leave behind family and friends and without those contacts you may feel isolated or bored. Do not forget, too, that if you make this change with your spouse or partner, one of you will eventually be left alone there. In many parts of the world – even in Europe – you will not find a free health service or even one of comparable quality at any price. You may be healthy in your 50s or 60s, but how will you cope with illness or disability in your 70s or 80s?

If you think the UK system is legalistic and bureaucratic, try dealing with an entirely foreign set of rules and civil servants – and in a foreign language. The culture you loved so much on holidays may seem very odd or even frightening when you have to live with it. Public transport may be difficult or non-existent. So make sure that the place you choose is somewhere you want to live, not just a place where you have had great holidays.

There are also legal and financial consequences to be aware of. In the 15 member states of the old European Union there should not be any problems about staying permanently as a retired resident. But the 12 new countries which have joined since 2004 may impose some restrictions for some years. It is vital to check first.

Countries outside the EU will probably impose restrictions on foreign nationals settling and retiring. Many demand a family connection or a certain (usually large) amount of money to be allowed to settle. In others you may find it is simply impossible to be guaranteed permanent residence.

BENEFITS FOR EXPATRIATES

Most state benefits are not paid to you if you live permanently abroad. The state retirement pension (but not Pension Credit) and widow's or bereavement benefits can be paid abroad, but in most countries they are not increased each year in line with inflation. Instead, they are frozen at the rate you were first paid the pension abroad. That rule does not apply in the 30 countries in the European Union and the European Economic Area and about 20 other countries with which Britain has a special agreement. But it does apply in the major emigration destinations of Australia, New Zealand, Canada and South Africa.

More than half the expatriate pensioner population lives outside the countries where the state pension is increased each year. Wherever you live, the pension will be paid in sterling and you will be responsible for the cost of conversion into the local currency.

War pensions – both for disablement and widows – are paid anywhere in the world at the rate they are paid in the UK, although extra amounts for constant attendance and exceptionally severe disablement are not paid abroad. No other benefits are paid to anyone who lives permanently outside the UK, with the one exception of the Winter Fuel Payment. This can paid throughout Europe as long as you move there after you have claimed it for at least one year while living in the UK.

PENSION IMPLICATIONS FOR PEOPLE LIVING ABROAD

If you are under pension age you can pay National Insurance contributions from abroad to make sure you get a full state pension when you do retire. Whether that is worth doing depends on how much state pension you have already earned. Remember that if you reach pension age from 6 April 2010 you only need 30 years of contributions to get a full pension anyway. If you have already paid enough contributions to get a full state pension, there is no point in paying any extra – and no point for men once they reach the pension age for women as credits are given automatically.

You can find out more from www.thepensionservice.gov.uk or by calling 0845 3000 168. If you work in a foreign country you will probably be paying into the local state pension system and, depending how long you work, you may be able to draw a local pension when you reach the pension age for that country.

A pension or annuity from your job, or one you have paid into yourself, can be paid abroad. If your pension or annuity is normally increased each year, that will continue. However, your pension or annuity will be paid in sterling and you will be responsible for the cost of converting it into the local currency. That also means that your actual income will vary with the exchange rate. Lots of small payments will mean paying a lot of bank charges. If you have several small pensions, it may be worth keeping a UK account to receive them all and then making one transfer to the country where you live.

TAX ISSUES FOR PEOPLE LIVING ABROAD

If you move to another country you will have to consider the local tax system as you will almost certainly have to pay tax on your world-wide income there. Income that still arises in the UK – from a pension or in a savings account or an investment, for example – will in theory still be taxable in the UK as well. The UK has agreements with many countries to prevent this double taxation. But you must check how it works to make sure you are not taxed twice.

These agreements normally provide for your income from a pension and investments in the UK to be taxed in the country where you live. In that case the interest and the pension can be paid gross, without deduction of UK tax. You will have to tell the pension provider, and the bank or building society where your money is deposited, that you now live abroad. Any income from rent on a UK property is always taxed in the UK and the Rent a Room scheme (see page 122) does not apply if you live abroad.

You will normally be entitled to the personal tax allowance, so if your income arising in the UK – including any rental income – is less than about £5,500 you will not have to pay tax on it.

Although it is fairly easy to identify where you live there is another concept in taxation which is much more difficult. It is called 'domicile'. At birth you inherit the domicile of your father. Once you reach 16 you can change your domicile by moving permanently to another country. So if you retire abroad and intend to stay there until you die, that country may become your domicile of choice. However, if you intend to stay for a long time in a country but still keep property or connections in the UK, you will not acquire domicile in your new country. Domicile can affect the way you are taxed on income and capital gains, and it is likely to affect your will and liability to inheritance tax.

Many countries, including many others in Europe, tax wealth during your lifetime, not just when you die. You should make sure you understand – and are happy with – these taxes for the country where you are planning to settle. In particular, check on the position of husbands and wives. The UK rule that transfers on death between spouses are free of tax may not apply. You should also let your heirs know what they will have to do when they finally come to sort out your financial affairs. Make sure you understand the local laws about wills. In many countries you cannot disinherit blood relatives in the way you can in the UK. Property outside that country may be dealt with separately, particularly if you do not establish 'domicile' in your new country. If you do not make a will, then sorting out your financial affairs may be very difficult for those you leave behind.

BUYING PROPERTY ABROAD

Buying a house or flat in the UK can be stressful enough. In another country, with a different legal system and a foreign language, it can be much worse. Even when it all goes well, there can be problems in continental Europe about exactly what title you have to the property and what rights others may have over your property. Local lawyers can be slipshod about such things and it is often much harder abroad to get any compensation.

In Spain, in particular, many British expats have bought their dream home only to find it turn into a nightmare. Even the luckier ones have had to pay out very large sums of money to developers building roads or drains nearby for new developments. Others have seen their home demolished.

You should be very careful too when buying new property. You are often asked to buy before the foundations have been dug and are rushed into a decision with no time to get advice or consider things carefully. Even when things go well, many new developments that pass muster as holiday homes are just not up to the job of being your own home to live in all the year round. It is usually better to find an established home that a local family has lived in and buy that, as you would in the UK.

Just about every country has some sort of tax or charge on property. Make sure you know what you are letting yourself in for. If you borrow money locally to buy the property but your income is still in sterling, as it will normally be, you run the extra risk of the exchange rate moving in the wrong direction, leaving you with a bigger bill. If you find the payments are hard to meet, local laws may allow far harsher ways to recover debts than in the UK.

RETAINING A FOOTHOLD IN THE UK

All these dangers and difficulties make it essential to have an escape route back home – at least for a while. So if you can afford to move abroad without selling your UK home, that is ideal.

One way to avoid selling up in the UK is to let out your home so that you can try out the new country and give yourself time to be sure you have avoided the legal and financial pitfalls. But remember that any rental income from your property will still be taxable in the UK. If you do return to the UK, bear in mind that you will be considered resident here for the whole tax year if you arrive before 6 October.

HEALTH ISSUES FOR PEOPLE MOVING ABROAD

Although we complain about the National Health Service, most of us are very glad of it from time to time. In particular, the NHS is almost unsurpassed for the treatment you get for urgent life-threatening conditions and is pretty well unique in being free at the point of need. In most other countries health services have to be paid for – either directly, through a specific tax or charge, or through compulsory or voluntary health insurance. So remember to check carefully with the country where you are going to live. Make sure that you are happy with the quality of the health care service and that you build in the cost of either the local taxes or of private health care insurance.

Remember too that as you get older those costs might rise considerably. In some countries you will be expected to take a family member with you to hospital to attend to your personal needs, such as feeding and going to the toilet – nurses may only provide nursing care. You may also find that you are discharged back home more quickly than you would be in the UK.

WHEN WILL I DIE?

Financial planning would be a lot simpler if we all knew when we were going to die. It would be the ultimate looking ahead. But we do not. One thing is clear though – on average people are living longer and longer and longer.

Every year the actuaries in the Office for National Statistics and the Government Actuary's Department crunch numbers and come up with what they call life tables, which tell us, on average, how long we have to live. Confusingly, there are several sets of tables based on different assumptions and different results depending where in the UK you live. This is all very interesting, but what most of us want to know is 'How long have I got?' or, to put it more bluntly, 'When will I die?'. And the short answer is later than the actuaries thought last year – because every year life expectancy gets longer.

Here are some numbers. For readers who like the technical aspects they are called 'cohort life expectancies'. They indicate a longer life than the alternative 'period life expectancies' which are often quoted. But the Government Actuary himself, no less, says they are considered more accurate for assessing how long an individual may expect to live.

Broadly speaking, in your 50s you can expect to live until 80 or 81 if you are a man and until 83 or 84 if you are a woman. Here are the details.

These figures – the cohort life tables – are supposed to take account of future increases in life expectancy. But they may not. Every time an actuary looks at the figures life seems to get longer. In Octo-

Age in 2008	Life expectancy	
	Men	Women
50	80.3	83.4
52	80.6	83.6
54	80.8	83.8
56	81.1	84.0
58	81.4	84.2
60	81.7	84.5
65	82.8	85.2
70	84.1	86.2
75	85.8	87.4
80	88.0	89.2
90	94.0	94.4

ber 2005 the Government Actuary Chris Daykin announced that he had stopped assuming that the length of life had some ultimate biological limit. In other words, the age we live to really could go on increasing forever – or, as he put it in actuaryspeak: 'Previous projections have assumed that rates of mortality would gradually diminish in the long term ... However ... the previous long-term assumptions have been too pessimistic. Thus ... the rates of improvement after 2029 are now assumed to remain constant.'

The figures in the table are also averages, or, more precisely, they give the time when half the population will have died. In other words, a woman of 56 has a 50:50 chance of dying around her 84th birthday. So even if you are average you have an even chance of living longer than these ages. Also, people in some parts of the UK and people with higher incomes generally live longer than average. So these figures are by no means upper limits. You could live until you are 120. You could outlive Jeanne Calment.

This is why we all have to be realistic about when we retire. If you hope – as we used to – to retire in your early 50s you could have 30 years of life to go, which is great, as long as you have the money to live those 30 years comfortably rather than just endure them. Even if you delay until you are 60 your pension will have to keep you on average for 23 years. If you wait until you are 70 your pension will only have to keep you for an average of about 15 years.

Retiring later is a double whizzy (that is the good version of a double whammy). First, your pension has to be stretched over fewer years. Second, you have had longer to pay into it so there will be more money to be stretched. So although we may all want to work for 30 years and retire for 30 more the arithmetic is against it. Just how much against is illustrated by the generous police service pension scheme. A police officer can retire on a full pension after 30 years' service whatever their age. So those who joined at the age of 20 can retire at 50. Others retire younger than 50 due to injury or ill health. Figures released early in 2008 showed that across Britain there were 165,000 serving police officers but pensions were being paid to nearly as many retired officers – 140,000. In some of the larger forces there were actually more officers getting a pension than there were serving police men and women.

Those figures illustrate very clearly the cost of people retiring at as young as 50 when people of that age have a life expectancy of 30 years or more. For those of us who have to fund our own futures, these figures provide rather indigestible food for thought.

Most of this book is about common sense.

Mid-life is a time when all those changes that we know will happen suddenly get a bit too close for comfort, and we begin, perhaps gradually, to realise that we cannot put them off forever. At 45 almost half of us have children living with us. By 55 that has fallen to one in 12, and by 65 to almost none. This can be a time when health begins to ebb away or at least those aches and pains creep up. But it can also be the start of a long period of freedom – from worry, from debt, from work itself. It just depends on your attitude and how well you plan. And if you do take it seriously and do a bit of planning, you could be at the start of the longest and best holiday of your life. ■

14

SOURCES OF FURTHER INFORMATION

HELP THE AGED

207–221 Pentonville Road
London
N1 9UZ
Tel: 020 7278 1114
Fax: 020 7239 1489
Email: info@helptheaged.org.uk
Website: www.helptheaged.org.uk
International charity working to
improve the lives of older people.
Funded by individuals, companies
and trusts, it carries out research,
campaigns for improvements in
policy and practice and provides
practical services to help older
people stay independent.

The Charity's services include:
Advice leaflets (some of which,
such as *Can You Claim It?* and *Making
a Will*, are referred to in the text of
this guide) can be downloaded from
the Help the Aged website or
ordered as a hard copy: call
0808 800 6565 (in Northern
Ireland 0808 808 7575).
Care Fees Advice Service
See www.helptheaged.org.uk or call
the freephone number 0500 76 74
76 (9am–5pm, Monday–Friday)
SeniorLine Freephone 0808 800
6565 (Northern Ireland 0808 808
7575), providing free, confidential and
impartial advice on benefits, care and
housing issues
Your Money Matters This
programme, run by Help the Aged
and Barclays for people of 60+, aims
to improve the skills, confidence and
financial situation of older people
by providing basic money
management training and debt

advice. See website for details,
including contact numbers for
local projects.
**Website
www.helptheaged.org.uk**
contains independent, impartial
information on benefits, pensions,
equity release, making a will, etc.

TAEN (The Age and Employment Network)

Tel: 020 7843 1590
Website: www.taen.org.uk
Supported by Help the Aged, TAEN
is a leading centre of expertise on
everything to do with age and
employment. It is also a campaigning
organisation, with a network of 250
member organisations, working for
better opportunities for older people
to continue working and learning.

OTHER ORGANISATIONS AND WEBSITES

BENEFITS
**Department for Work
and Pensions**
Winter Fuel Payment
Tel: 08459 15 15 15.
Website:
www.thepensionservice.gov.uk/
winterfuel/home.asp

Entitledto
Website: www.entitledto.com
Independent advice on benefits
entitlement.

Pension Credit helpline
Credit helpline: 0800 99 1234
(0808 100 6165 in
Northern Ireland).

Council Tax Benefit and Housing Benefit can be claimed at the same time as Pension Credit.

Pension Credit calculator
Website:
www.direct.gov.uk/en/MoneyTaxAnd Benefits/.../On_a_low_income/DG_ 10018692
(See also entitledto.com)

CARING
Caring for a Parent in Later Life, by Judith Cameron, is a companion title in the LifeGuides series to *Making Your Money Work for Your Future*. Written for those whose parents have reached an aged where they are less able to cope with life, the guide looks at what type of care is available, housing options and home adaptations, pensions, benefits, legal matters, health, hospitals and more. Price: £8.99. Available via www.helptheaged.org.uk or by calling 020 7239 1946.

Carers UK
Tel: 0808 808 7777; 020 7922 8000
Website: www.carersuk.org.
Advice on caring, including care assessments and Carer's Allowance.

CASH MACHINES
Website: www.link.co.uk
To check which ones in your area do not charge for withdrawals.

CREDIT CARDS
Website:
www.moneysavingexpert.com.
Up-to-date guidance on credit cards.

CREDIT DETAILS PROTECTION (see page 171)
CIFAS
Website: www.cifas.org.uk

Equifax
Tel: 0800 783 9421
This is the credit reference agency that operates the protection system.

Protective.registrationuk
Email:
protective.registrationuk@equifax.com

CREDIT REFERENCE AGENCIES
Callcredit
Tel: 0113 244 1555 or
0870 060 1414
Website:
www.callcredit.co.uk/consumer

Equifax
Tel: 0800 783 9421 or
0845 600 1772
Website: www.equifax.co.uk

Experian
Tel: 0800 656 9000 or
0870 241 6212
Website: www.experian.co.uk

DEBT COUNSELLING
Citizens Advice
For local office see www.nacab.org.uk or local phone book

Consumer Credit Counselling Service
Tel: 0800 138 1111
Website: www.cccs.co.uk

National Debtline
Tel: 0808 808 4000
Website: www.nationaldebtline.co.uk

DIVORCE
Resolution
Tel: 01689 820272
Website: www.resolution.org.uk
Organisation comprising more than
5,000 registered solicitors specialising
in efficient and amicable divorce.

EMPLOYMENT
Working at 50+, by Malcolm Hornby,
is a companion title in the LifeGuides
series to *Making Your Money Work
for Your Future*. Written specifically
for those in mid-life who are looking
for a job or exploring other ways
to boost their income, it contains
practical advice on every aspect
of finding and staying in employment,
including how to identify and
overcome age discrimination.
Price: £8.99. Available via
www.helptheaged.org.uk or
by calling 020 7239 1946.

**Equality and Human Rights
Commission**
Website:
www.equalityhumanrights.com
Advice on discrimination.

Government
Website: www.direct.gov.uk
The gateway to more and more
official information. Its search engine
will usually take you to the
information you need.
Website:
www.direct.gov.uk/en/Employment/
Employees/Pay/DG_10027201

www.hmrc.gov.uk/nmw
National Minimum Wage helpline:
0845 6000 678

Website:
www.workingforyourself.co.uk
for HMRC advice on self-employment.

EMPLOYMENT TRIBUNALS
**ACAS (Advisory, Conciliation
and Arbitration Service)**
Helpline: 0845 7474747
Website: www acas.og.uk
Publicly funded body that offers advice
on employment rights and legislation.

Tribunals Service
Website:
www.employmenttribunals.gov.uk
Government agency that provides all
the documentation and information
required to take a claim to an
employment tribunal.

Citizens Advice
For local office see www.nacab.org.uk
or local phone book.

ENERGY-SAVING
Energy Saving Trust
Website: www.energysavingtrust.org.uk

ENERGY SUPPLIERS
Energywatch
Website: www.energywatch.org.uk
to find the cheapest supplier.
Energywatch will cease to exist in
2008, after which try www.ncc.org.uk
(National Consumer Council).

Moneysavingexpert
Website:
www.moneysavingexpert.com

Lots of tips on saving money, including the right time to switch suppliers and information on credit cards.

EQUITY RELEASE
Safe Home Income Plans
Website: www.ship-ltd.org
Download the useful checklist.

FREEPHONE (0800) NUMBERS
Saynoto0870
Website: www.saynoto0870.com
to find free telephone numbers for businesses that try to make you pay to call them.

HOME REPAIRS
Home Improvement Agencies
(a.k.a. **Staying Put Agency** or **Care & Repair**)
Website: www.housingcare.org
Charitable organisations that help older or disabled people to repair or improve their homes. Website offers useful advice on how to manage where you live. For your local office ask the local social services department or use www.housingcare.org./search/home-improvement-agency.aspx

INHERITANCE TAX
HM Revenue & Customs
Inheritance Tax and Probate helpline: 0845 302 0900
Website:
www.hmrc.gov.uk/cto/iht.htm
www.hmrc.gov.uk/cto/customerguide/page15.htm (thresholds)

PENSIONS
Pension Service
Website:
www.thepensionservice.gov.uk/atoz/atozdetailed/pensiontracing.asp
(pension tracing)
www.thepensionservice.gov.uk/statepensiondeferral/choices.asp
(pension deferral)
www.thepensionservice.gov.uk
(advice on pensions when moving abroad)

Pensions Advisory Service
Tel. (helpline): 0845 601 2923
Website:
www.pensionsadvisoryservice.org.uk;
(pension tracing)
This independent non-profit organisation provides free information, advice and guidance on the whole spectrum of pensions: state, company, personal and stakeholder schemes.

Unclaimed Assets Register
Website: www.uar.co.uk
For tracing unclaimed pensions (fee charged).

RENTING OUT ROOMS
Rent a Room scheme
Website: www.direct.gov.uk
For information, search on 'letting rooms in your home'.

STAMP DUTY
Disadvantaged Areas Relief
Website: www.hmrc.gov.uk/so/dar/dar-search.htm
For information on areas where the government applies lower stamp duty charges on home transactions.

TAX
HM Revenue & Customs
Form CF9 (to change from married woman's reduced-rate NI contributions to full-rate contributions, in order to achieve a better state pension) can be downloaded from www.hmrc.gov.uk/forms/cf9.pdf

Form R85 (for non-taxpayers, to prevent tax being deducted from savings) can be downloaded from www.hmrc.gov.uk/forms/r85.pdf

Website: www.hmrc.gov.uk/p2 for explanation of **Notice of Coding**.

Tel: 0845 980 0645 to register for receiving **interest gross** (i.e. without tax deducted).

Website: www.hmrc.gov.uk/taxback for useful information. Download form **R40** (one for each past tax year) to use for **reclaiming tax** from www.hmrc.gov.uk/forms/r40.pdf. Tel. (helpline): 0845 077 6543 to find out about claiming overpaid tax back.

Self-assessment helpline: 0845 9000 444.

Self-assessment helpsheet IR222, for advice on business expenses and capital allowances, etc.: via www.hmrc.gov.uk/helpsheets/ir222. pdf or via HMRC order line: 08459 000 404

TAX QUERIES
(people on low incomes)
TaxAid
Tel: 0845 120 3779 (10am–noon, Mondays–Thursdays)
Website: www.taxaid.org.uk

Tax Help for Older People
Tel: 0845 601 3321
Website: www.taxvol.org.uk

Low Incomes Tax Reform
Website: www.litrg.org.uk

TAX CREDITS
HM Revenue & Customs
Tel: 0845 300 3900; Northern Ireland 0845 603 2000 .
to request claim pack.
(See also www.entitledto.com)
Website:
www.hmrc.gov.uk/menus/credits.htm. for further information.

INDEX

HELP THE AGED

Help the Aged is an international charity dedicated to creating a world where older people can live their lives free from poverty, isolation, neglect and ageism. We also work to prevent deprivation among future generations of older people, by improving prospects for employment, health and well-being so that dependence in later life is reduced.

The Charity's unique understanding of older people's needs enables it to raise public awareness of issues affecting older people in the UK and overseas, campaign for changes in policy and practice nationally and regionally, and provide practical support to help disadvantaged older people live independent lives. Independent of government, it is funded by individuals, companies and trusts. It also operates advice lines, publishes information and guidance, and runs a nationwide network of charity shops.

With your support, we can achieve even more. Could **you** help **us** to help older people, by:

- donating unwanted goods to your local Help the Aged shop?
- recycling your old mobile phone, toner cartridges or glasses to raise vital funds?
- selling raffle tickets or contributing to one of our appeals?
- making a regular donation by direct debit or online at www.helptheaged.org.uk?
- applying for a Help the Aged credit card?
- signing up to Sponsor a Grandparent overseas?

To find out more about supporting Help the Aged, visit **www.helptheaged.org.uk**